Palladio and Prosecco

Art Walks in the Veneto

Copyright © 2020 by Janet Faulkner Chapman
ISBN 978-0-9976312-1-0

Interior design by Val Sherer, Personalized Publishing Services
Cover & maps by Judy Baker, Brandvines

All Rights Reserved. No part of this book may be copied or reproduced by any means, electronic or mechanical, including photocopying, recording, or any information storage and retrieval system, without prior permission in writing by the publisher.

To Harry

Acknowledgements

The Veneto is one of the most beautiful places in the world. I was inspired to learn about Andrea Palladio and visit the Veneto by a childhood memory of a photograph of 'La Rotonda'. But I might not have written this book without the support, encouragement and inspiration from my friends and colleagues. I am extremely grateful for the reviews and editorial assistance from my friends, including Steven Baker, Robert Pucci, Patty Dryer, Ciji Ware, Donna Bachle, Michele Benjamin, Joseph Cozza, Cheryl Popp and many others.

I was inspired to return to Vicenza by my dear friend Patty Dryer and her daughter Allie who studied architecture there.

I might not have considered Padova without the advice and insights of Steven Baker who studied in Padova and insisted I visit the Scrovegni Chapel and take the trip along the Brenta Canal.

I was educated about Verona and the Prosecco region by Chefs Alessandro Spaziani-Montagna and Monika Troggler, the husband and wife team who have an incredible restaurant, Sandrino, in Sausalito, CA. Alessandro also taught me about Cartizze, and how to correctly pronounce Valdobbiadene, the heart of the Prosecco region.

And I got valuable information from Natalia Franca, our wonderful AirBnB hostess in Bassano del Grappa. In addition to having a sensational apartment rental (Appartamenti Ponte-Vecchio) with a view of Ponte degli Alpini and the Brenta River, Natalia gave us a wealth of information about a wonderful restaurant in Bassano (Birreria Ottone) and other tips.

This book would not have been possible without the extraordinary design and formatting skills of Val Sherer, Personalized Publishing Services, who put this book together and taught me so much, and the design skills of Judy Baker (Brandvines) who designed and executed the walking tour maps and the cover. Kelley Way (www.kawaylaw.com/) provided expert legal assistance.

I also wish to acknowledge the Bay Area Independent Publishers Association (BAIPA) for providing such an excellent forum and resources for the independent publishing community.

And last, but not least, thank you to my husband Harry. Thanks to the seminars he conducted in Rome every year, sponsored by the Technology Transfer Institute of Italy, we were able to spend many weeks in Italy and be inspired by *'la dolce vita'* every day.

Contents

Introduction ix

How to Use this Book. xii

Walking Tour #1
Vicenza City Center 3

Walking Tour #2
Vicenza Teatro Olimpico
and Palazzo Chiericati 17

Walking Tour #3
Villa Rotonda, and Villa Valmarana ai Nani . . 31

Walking Tour #4
Verona Highlights 43

Walking Tour #5
Verona's Basilica—San Zeno Maggiore
with the Mantegna altarpiece and Piazza Bra . 53

Walking Tour # 6
Padova (Padua) the home of The Scrovegni Chapel
with Giotto's frescoes 65

Walking Tour #7
Highlights of Padova 79

Walking Tour #8
Padova to Venezia—
Cruising on the Brenta Canal 91

Walking Tour #9
Bassano del Grappa and Palladio's Ponte degli Alpini
and Asolo and Palladio's Villa Barbaro in Maser 109

Walking Tour #10
Valdobbiadene and the Prosecco Wine Road . . 125

My Favorite Restaurants in the Veneto 133

About the Author 135

Palladio Prosecco: Art Walks in the Veneto

Introduction

In 1870, Thomas Jefferson, the third President of the United States, wrote to his friend and Presidential successor, James Madison:

"We are sadly at a loss here for a Palladio."[1]

Jefferson was referring to *I Quattro Libri dell'Archittectura* (The Four Books of Architecture) written by Andrea Palladio in 1570. These books became a kind of 'bible' for architects worldwide and brought Palladio lasting fame. Jefferson owned three sets of *Quattro Libri* and his designs of his beloved home Monticello, as well as the Rotunda at the University of Virginia (UVA) were greatly influenced by Palladio.

In fact, Jefferson's Monticello and UVA's Rotunda were modeled in part after one of Palladio's masterpieces, Villa Capra-La Rotonda, just outside Vicenza, Italy.

This is more interesting and relevant than what might appear—if you visit Washington, D.C. or London, England, for example, you may notice many domes, columns and arched windows. You might think that these are Greco-Roman architectural influences and you'd be correct but these are also the hallmarks of Palladian architecture.

For example, Palladio's drawings of ancient Roman monuments, presented in the fourth book of *I Quattro Libri*, greatly influenced the architects of some of America's most significant and beautiful public buildings  of the late-nineteenth century. These include the White

---

[1] Peter D'Epiro and Mary Desmond Pinkowish, Sprezzatura: 50 Ways Italian Genius Shaped The World, (Anchor Books, New York) 2001

House and the original West Wing of the National Gallery of Art in Washington, D.C.

Palladio's principles of symmetry, elegance and harmonious design were also influential in England as a result of the architect Inigo Jones (1573-1652). Jones visited Italy and acquired a copy of *I Quattro Libri*. One of his best-known works, still standing, is the Banqueting House in Whitehall, London, shown in this photograph.

In my opinion, this building looks like it was inspired by Palazzo Chiericati, one of Palladio's masterpieces in Vicenza that we will visit in Walking Tour #2.

Andrea Palladio was born in Padova (Padua) in 1508. His real name was Andrea di Pietro della Gondola. As a young man, he was apprenticed to a sculptor in Padova. Then he moved to Vicenza and enrolled in the guild of stonemasons. He was initially employed as a mason in workshops specializing in monuments and decorative sculpture.

When he moved to Vicenza, he met Count Giangiorgio Trissino who became his patron and gave him his start. In 1541, Count Trissino took Palladio to Rome where he began to carefully study ancient buildings.

This time in Rome was the beginning of a transformation of Palladio into one of the greatest architects of 16th century northern Italy. Trissino

Introduction

recognized his abilities and bestowed on him the name of Palladio, apparently as a reference to 'Pallas Athena,' the Greek goddess of Wisdom.

His designs for palaces (palazzi), notably the Villa Rotonda just outside Vicenza, made his reputation in Vicenza and Venezia as an architect and builder of buildings that were elegant and aesthetically pleasing. That said, his books titled *I Quattro Libri dell'Architettura* that he wrote in 1570 made him one of the most influential figures in Western architecture. Palladio's immortality as an architect is in large part based on his publication of the *Quattro Libri,* which greatly influenced building design the world over, but especially in Italy, Great Britain, and the United States.

In 1994, the city of Vicenza and the 23 Palladian buildings within the city was named a UNESCO World Heritage Site. In 1996, 21 additional villas within the Veneto region were added to the UNESCO Registry. [2]

I was a child when I first saw a photograph of La Rotonda. I was captivated by this gorgeous building and, finally in 2010, paid my first visit to Vicenza to see it. Thus began my love affair with Palladio and the more I researched, the more I realized just how extraordinary and influential he was.

---

[2] http://whc.unesco.org/en/list/712

How to use this book

I begin almost every walking tour at a train station in each city I visit so it's easy to find. Most of the walks are within, or adjacent to, the Central Historical District or Centro Storico in each city. Given the title of this guide, you've probably surmised that the tours are mostly designed for walkers; however, because the Veneto is a large area, I've had to include driving directions to some of the cities and monuments. Accordingly, I've included some tips for driving and places to park. The tours each take several hours; I'd allow for half a day for most and longer for some.

Because touring is thirsty work, I've also included tips on nearby cafes because one may often be in need of a meal or at least a refreshing caffe or a prosecco, depending on the time of day. Look for these in the sections boxed in Red and titled "Ready for a Pick-me-Up?"

And, for those who do have additional time to spend, I've added some of my personal favorite sites to visit along the way. Look for these in the sections boxed in Blue and titled "If You Have the Time…."

What's not here

Venezia is obviously the most famous and heavily visited tourist attraction in the Veneto. In fact, many tourists have no idea that Venezia is even part of the Veneto. Because there is so much more to the Veneto than Venezia, this book will not go there, except tangentially in Walking Tour #8, The Brenta Canal.

Nevertheless, Venezia is a wonderful magical place and it's filled with beautiful vistas as well as global treasures, so please make time to see them on your own.

Introduction

City Passes

Several of the major cities, such as Vicenza, Padova and Verona, that we'll visit have special programs that enable tourists to visit selected museums and cultural sites at discounted prices. I have noted the museums and cultural attractions that allow the pass in each walking tour.

What follows are art walks that are my personal favorites in the Veneto.

The Walking Tours

1. Vicenza City Center
2. Vicenza—Palladio's Teatro Olimpico and Palazzo Chiericati
3. Villa La Rotonda, Villa Valmarana ai Nani, and Monte Berico
4. Verona Highlights
5. Verona's Basilica—San Zeno Maggiore and Piazza Bra
6. Padova Must-See—Scrovegni Chapel
7. Padova Highlights in Palladio's Birthplace
8. Padova to Venezia—Cruising on the Brenta Canal
9. Bassano del Grappa and Palladio's Ponte degli Alpini, and Asolo and Palladio's Villa Barbaro in Maser
10. Valdobbiadene and the Prosecco Wine Road

The Photographs in this book

The vast majority of photos in the book were taken by me, and are beloved mementos of my trips. I have listed the other photos and their respective sources below. All photographs unless otherwise indicated (below) are covered under copyright-Janet Chapman (2010-2017)©

Introduction: photograph of Banqueting House in Whitehall, Wikipedia article on Banqueting House, Whitehall
(https://en.wikipedia.org/wiki/Banqueting_House,_Whitehall). This picture is licensed under the Creative Commons Attribution-Share Alike 3.0 Unported license (https://creativecommons.org/licenses/by-sa/3.0/)

Walking Tour #1: Palazzo del Capitaniato, Wikipedia article on Palazzo del Capitanio (Vicenza) https://commons.wikimedia.org/wiki/File:Palazzo_del_Capitanio_(Vicenza).jpg
This picture is licensed under the Creative Commons Attribution-Share Alike 4.0 International license.

Walking Tour #3: Basilica di S. Maria di Monte Berico, Wikipedia article on Monte Berico https://en.wikipedia.org/wiki/Monte_Berico
This picture is licensed under the Creative Commons Attribution-Share Alike 4.0 International license.

Walking Tour #7: Prato della Valle, Wikipedia article on Prato della Valle https://en.wikipedia.org/wiki/Prato_della_Valle
This picture is licensed under the Creative Commons Attribution-Share Alike 4.0 International license.

Walking Tour #8: Villa Widmann-Foscari, article on Villa Widmann-Foscari
https://en.wikipedia.org/wiki/Villa_Widmann
This picture is licensed under the Creative Commons Attribution-Share Alike 3.0 Unported license.

Palladio and Prosecco
Art Walks in the Veneto

Walking Tour #1
Vicenza City Center

Any review of Palladian architecture and buildings really should begin in Vicenza as the city has the largest concentration of 'still-standing' Palladian structures. Vicenza has fully embraced its role as the 'City of Palladio' and has many markers inside the old city pointing out Palladio's buildings. Vicenza was designated a UNESCO World Heritage Site in 1994 for its extensive array of twenty-three surviving Palladian buildings.[3]

Walking Tour #1 starts at the Vicenza train station located at the intersection of Viale Venezia and Viale Roma. If you're driving, there are multiple parking garages such as Verdi close by the station. Exit from either the train station or Verdi Parcheggio (parking garage) onto Viale Roma. Follow Viale Roma walking through the Campo Marzio for several blocks until you reach Piazzale de Gasperi. Turn right and go under the gate at the edge of the old city.

This is the Torrione di Porta Castello, or the Porta Castello Tower that was built in 1343 as a medieval sentry structure.

---

[3] https://whc.unesco.org/en/documents/112697

As you cross under the gate, you'll be on Corso Andrea Palladio, the street that runs through the center of the historic city.

As you walk along the Corso, you'll notice a variety of aging structures, some of which are Palladian—or at least Palladian-inspired, on either side of the street along with beautiful shops and cafes. For example, at the eastern edge of Piazza Castello, you'll see Palazzo Thiene Bonin Longare (designed by Palladio but actually built by Vicenzo Scamozzi) and Palazzo Capra on either side of the street.

Vicenzo Scamozzi (1548-1616) was a slightly later architect whose work is sometimes mistaken for Palladio's.

If You Have the Time

As you reach the next intersection on Corso A. Palladio, turn right and walk a couple of short blocks to Piazza del Duomo, the site of the Santa Maria Annunciata Cathedral. The building of the Cathedral began in 1482 and was completed in 1580. Palladio designed the dome of the church, and possibly the north doorway. The Cathedral is the main Catholic Church for Vicenza and also the seat of the Bishop of Vicenza. It's a beautiful building in the Gothic style. The Cathedral was heavily damaged by bombs in World War II but it has been restored. Spend a few moments inside the church to admire its Gothic structure and beautiful chapels. The Cathedral is also on top of an archeological site dating from the Roman era. Upon leaving the Cathedral, turn right and return to Corso A. Palladio.

Vicenza City Center

Turn right onto Corso A. Palladio and continue toward the center, passing by Palazzo Valmarano Braga Rosa on a side street on the left (Corso Fogazzarro). Palazzo Valmarano Braga was designed by Palladio in 1565 utilizing an existing location in Vicenza. It's a grand building fronted by columns that was heavily damaged during World War II but was restored after the war and has apartments available for rent.

Continuing on Corso Palladio, you'll pass by Palazzo Pojana or Poiana on the right. This is attributed to Palladio from about 1561. It certainly resembles Palladio's design style with the symmetric windows and columns but there is no documentation confirming this. Still, it's an example of Palladio's widespread influence.

Turn right onto Contra Cavour passing another villa on the corner, Villa Trissino Baston. Although it has Palladian influences, this building was designed by Vicenzo Scamozzi. Scamozzi was famous in his own right and this building is considered one of his masterpieces. He actually finished several Palladian buildings including Teatro Olimpico, a marvelous building that we'll visit in Walking Tour #2.

Continue on Contra Cavour turning left at the next intersection and walking toward the Piazza dei Signori. Ahead of you is the magnificent Basilica Palladiana (1545-1617), also known as the Palazzo della Ragione. This was Palladio's first major commission for a public building and it became known as 'Palladiana' after completion.

It's a remarkable building with its extraordinary copper domed roof, columns, arches and statuary on the roof, indicative of later Palladian hallmarks.

The Basilica (an ancient term for public building, not necessarily a religious building) is considered Vicenza's cultural center and includes the Museo del Gioello (Jewelry Museum), that opened in 2014. I wasn't able to visit it when I was in Vicenza but I've included a link to it. https://www.inexhibit.com/mymuseum/basilica-palladiana-vicenza-jewelry-museum/

Take a few moments to walk around the building. It's beautiful as well as functional. There are shops and restaurants within the surrounding arcade as well as an exhibition hall that provides a great space for special exhibits.

As you walk along the arcade, you'll notice a graceful wide staircase leading to the upper floor. I've been told that there is an open-air café that is accessible during the summer. However, as you notice in the photo, there is a locked grillwork gate at the top of the stairs and I've never been to Vicenza when the upper level is open.

As you walk to the right side of the Basilica, you'll see Palladio's statue. It was created by Vincenzo Gajassi and titled 'Monument to Palladio.' The statue was commissioned by Francesco Bressan and donated to the City of Vicenza in 1859. This was Gajassi's last commission and is considered his masterpiece. Gajassi died in 1861.

He looks like he might be pensively contemplating this famous edifice.

Walking Tour #1

As you turn to the main piazza, notice the clock tower adjacent to the Basilica. This is the Torre Bissara.

It was part of the original building that was here before Palladio's work. Originally, there were actually two separate buildings. In 1545, the city leaders, who were presumably influenced by Giangorgio Trissini, a wealthy citizen of Vicenza who was Palladio's patron in his early years. The clock tower was part of one of the original buildings that were built in the 13th century although the tower itself was referenced as existing in the 12th century.

During World War II, the Basilica and the Tower were severely damaged by Allied bombs. The tower and the dome partially collapsed but a restoration project began in 2002 to bring the buildings back to their full glory.

The Piazza is the major gathering area in Vicenza and is frequently filled with stalls and carts; various market days can be focused on food, or clothing as well as antiques. If you're lucky enough to encounter one of them, take some time to explore the wares and talk to the merchants.

Vicenza City Center

Across the Piazza from Basilica Palladiano is the beautiful Palazzo del Capitaniato, also known as Loggia del Capitanio. This building was designed by Palladio in 1565. The palazzo is currently used by Vicenza's town council. At one end of the Piazza you can also see a pillar with a lion on top of it, symbolizing that Vicenza was once part of the Venetian Republic.

When you decide to leave the wonderful Piazza dei Signori and the Basilica Palladiana, cross to the far end on the left and follow Contra Moretti back to Corso Palladio. Cross the Corso and follow the street named Contra Porti. On the left at the next intersection, you'll come to Palazzo Barbaran da Porto, the home of the Palladian Museum.

Before you head to the Palladian Museum, consider heading to the Vicenza Tourist Bureau, which is located at the end of Corso Palladio at the Piazza Matteotti, and purchasing a Biglietto Unico Museum Card. The card is a combination ticket that allows access to 8 different museums including the Palladian Museum that we will visit on this walking tour as well as the Teatro Olimpico and the Palazzo Chiericati that we will visit on Walking Tour #2. In 2017, the price was € 15,00.

Palazzo Barbarano, The Palladian Museum

Hours: Tuesday–Sunday, 10:00A.M.–6:00P.M.
Price: € 8,00 or included in the Biglietto Unico Museum Card

The Palladian Museum, opened in 2012, is located in Palazzo Barbarano, a building that Palladio actually built in 1570 for a Vicenzan aristocrat, Montano Barbarano. It has been the home of the International Center for Architectural Studies (CISA) since 1958; CISA is the group that oversees the museum and has funded and handled the restoration of the structure.

The palazzo and other noteworthy buildings in the historic center of Vicenza have very helpful signage in Italian and English that give you some of the key dates and background to enhance your understanding.

Palazzo Barbarano is an interesting building in that Palladio had to figure out how to design it carefully because it had to be constructed between existing buildings. The result is an asymmetrical structure. And unusually, Palladio lived long enough to complete the interior decoration as well as the exterior construction. The building has been beautifully restored into a modern exhibition space for the public and for architectural scholars who come to do research and share information. While it's centered on Palladio, other architects can be featured as well.

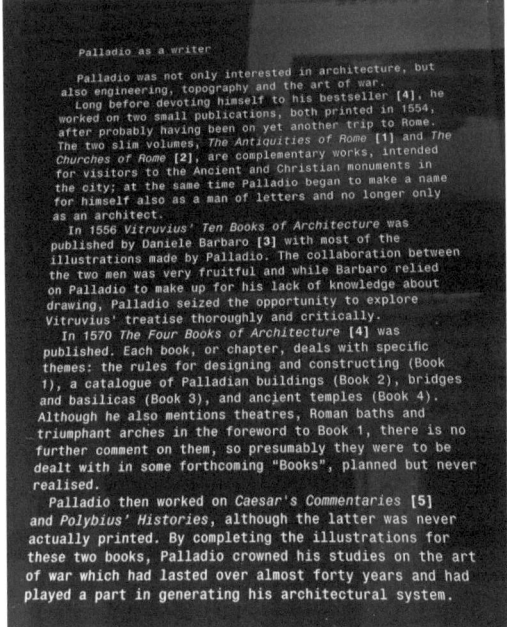

Palladio as a writer

Palladio was not only interested in architecture, but also engineering, topography and the art of war.
Long before devoting himself to his bestseller [4], he worked on two small publications, both printed in 1554, after probably having been on yet another trip to Rome. The two slim volumes, *The Antiquities of Rome* [1] and *The Churches of Rome* [2], are complementary works, intended for visitors to the Ancient and Christian monuments in the city; at the same time Palladio began to make a name for himself also as a man of letters and no longer only as an architect.
In 1556 *Vitruvius' Ten Books of Architecture* [3] was published by Daniele Barbaro with most of the illustrations made by Palladio. The collaboration between the two men was very fruitful and while Barbaro relied on Palladio to make up for his lack of knowledge about drawing, Palladio seized the opportunity to explore Vitruvius' treatise thoroughly and critically.
In 1570 *The Four Books of Architecture* [4] was published. Each book, or chapter, deals with specific themes: the rules for designing and constructing (Book 1), a catalogue of Palladian buildings (Book 2), bridges and basilicas (Book 3), and ancient temples (Book 4). Although he also mentions theatres, Roman baths and triumphant arches in the foreword to Book 1, there is no further comment on them, so presumably they were to be dealt with in some forthcoming "Books", planned but never realised.
Palladio then worked on *Caesar's Commentaries* [5] and *Polybius' Histories*, although the latter was never actually printed. By completing the illustrations for these two books, Palladio crowned his studies on the art of war which had lasted over almost forty years and had played a part in generating his architectural system.

The first floor has a bookstore and beautifully lit display spaces showing sections of Palladio's Four Books on Architecture—the *Quattro Libri*—that he published in 1570. All explanations and descriptions are in Italian as well as English.

As you head up the beautiful staircase, you'll note a visual timeline of Palladio's life and key accomplishments, all designed to help set context and help you better understand Palladio's genius.

On the second floor, there are a series of rooms highlighting various aspects of Palladio's style and architectural improvements.

For example, Palladio figured out how to reduce the cost of construction of some of his signature embellishments such as the columns. Instead of constructing them completely from stone, he developed the technique shown in the photo of using brick and other materials for the interior and cladding only the exterior of the column in more expensive stone.

In addition, there are stunning scale models of some of Palladio's most famous buildings such as this one of the Basilica shown here.

There are also 'holograms' of various architectural experts explaining key elements of Palladio's work and why he was so influential.

There are also drawings done by Palladio as well as

Vicenza City Center

some of his papers. Many of these materials are on loan from the Royal Institute of British Architects, which has an agreement with the museum.

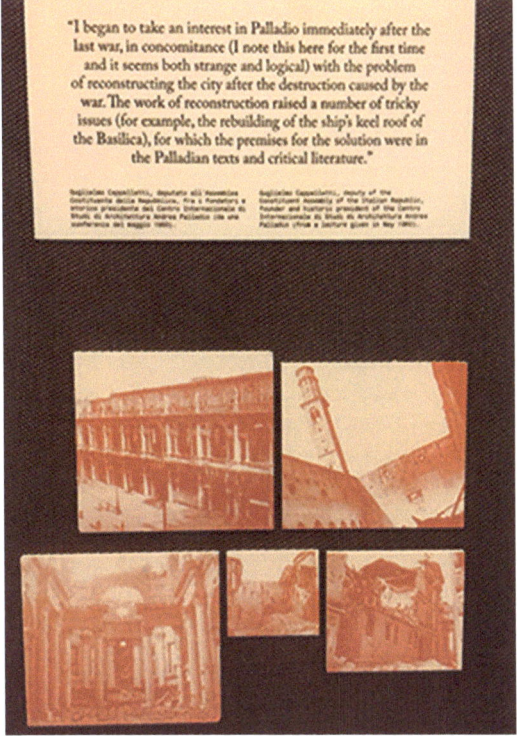

The museum is fascinating and well worth spending a few hours. As you climb up or down the staircase, take note of the interior courtyard, which has a mulberry tree growing there. This is a symbol of Vicenza's former silk industry, the source of much of the wealth of some of Palladio's patrons.

As you exit the bookstore on the main level, take a moment to note some of the original founders of the museum. One of the photographs caught my eye.

Sir Anthony Blunt of England was a well-known art historian and author of well-received books on various French and Italian artists, and, at one time, the Queen's Curator of Pictures. He became notorious in 1964 after he confessed to being a Soviet spy. He was one of the so-called 'Cambridge Five', a group of graduates of Cambridge University who worked in various capacities in the British Government, including British Intelligence during World War II. I'm speculating that this may be a reason why the Museum was able to arrange for the transfer of many of Palladio's drawings and papers that were archived in Britain.

After spending several hours in Palladian Museum, head back along Corso Palladio until you arrive at Piazza dei Signori for a well-deserved break.

Ready for a Pick-me-Up?

Museum visits can be exhilarating as well as exhausting. As you cross the piazza, head back toward the Basilica. If you need a break, a wonderful café and restaurant is immediately adjacent. Garibaldi's is a gorgeous place for a break and allows you to sit and sip your prosecco or an Aperol spritzer with a full view of the Basilica and all the happenings in the piazza. On a sunny day, there are few more delightful places to relax and enjoy this part of Italy.

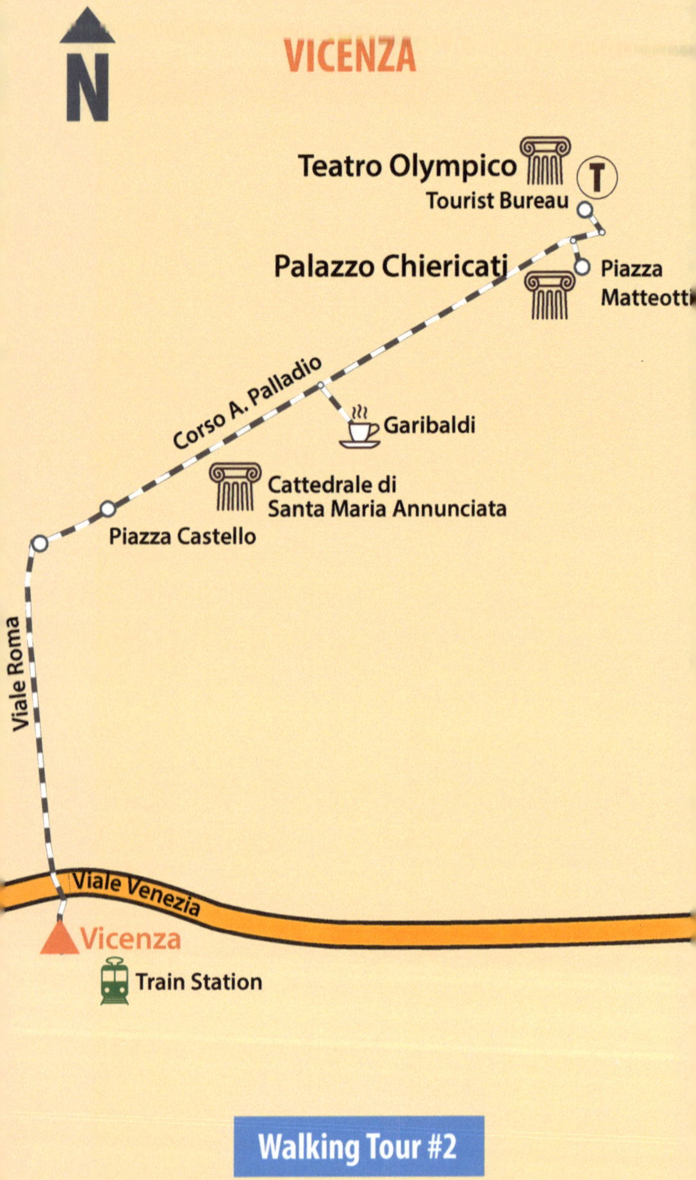
N
VICENZA
Teatro Olympico
T
Tourist Bureau
Palazzo Chiericati
Piazza
Matteotti
Corso A. Palladio
Garibaldi
Cattedrale di
Santa Maria Annunciata
Piazza Castello
Viale Roma
Viale Venezia
Vicenza
Train Station
Walking Tour #2

Walking Tour #2

Vicenza Teatro Olimpico and Palazzo Chiericati

Walking tour #2 starts at the Vicenza train station located at the intersection of Viale Venezia and Viale Roma. If you're driving, there are multiple parking garages such as Verdi close by the station. Exit from either the train station or Verdi Parcheggio (parking garage) onto Viale Roma. Follow Viale Roma walking through the Campo Marzio for several blocks until you reach Piazzale de Gasperi. Turn right and go under the gate at the edge of the old city.

This is the Torrione di Porta Castello, or the Porta Castello Tower that was built in 1343 as a medieval sentry structure.

As you cross under the gate, you'll be on Corso Andrea Palladio, the street that runs through the center of the historic city.

As you walk along the Corso, you'll notice a variety of aging structures, some of which are Palladian, on either side of the street along with beautiful shops and cafes. It is a beautiful street for strolling, window-shopping or real shopping.

When you reach the far end of Corso Palladio, you will reach one of the most famous of Palladio's buildings; Teatro Olimpico (the Olympic Theatre), considered by many to be one of Palladio's masterpieces.

Before you enter the Teatro Olimpico, I'd advise you to first consider heading to the Vicenza Tourist Bureau, which is located next door. At the Tourist Bureau, you can purchase a Biglietto Unico Museum Card that I described in Walking Tour #1.

The Biglietto Unico Museum Card is a combination ticket that allows access to eight different museums including Teatro Olimpico and the Palazzo Chiericati that we will visit on this tour. In 2017, the price was € 15,00.

Teatro Olimpico

Vicenza Teatro Olimpico and Palazzo Chiericati

Hours: Tuesday–Sunday, closed on Monday
September to June: 9:00a.m.–5:00p.m.
July and August: 10:00a.m.–6:00p.m.
Price: € 11,00 or included in the
Biglietto Unico Museum Card

Teatro Olimpico, on Piazza Matteotti, was built in 1585 and was Palladio's last building. It is reputed to be the oldest enclosed theatre in the world. Palladio was responsible for the design of the theatre but he died before it was finished. Vincenzio Scamozza, another prominent architect who worked on other Palladian buildings as noted in Walking Tour #1, completed the Theatre.

Palladio was a founding member of the Accademia Olimpica (Olympic Academy) begun in 1555. Teatro Olimpico became the permanent home of the Accademia. The Accademia's purpose is to promote the cultural life of Vicenza through intellectual discussions, publications and teaching activities. And of course, the primary activity of the Accademia is to preserve the Teatro and promote its public use. While the Teatro is the center of the Accademia, there were other buildings but allied bombs in World War II destroyed these.

Palladio designed the theatre to be reminiscent of old Roman and Greek amphitheatres. The theatre's opening play was 'Oedipus Rex' by Sophocles.

The stage set, while designed by Palladio, was actually built by his son and by the architect Scamozza to represent the city of Thebes. Scamozza was the one to figure out the amazing perspective of the set that consists of seven hallways, giving the impression of looking down the streets of Thebes. It's miraculous that this stage set still exists given its construction of stucco and wood. Oil lamps that were designed by Scamozza originally lighted the theatre, making its intact existence all the more remarkable.

Enter the theatre by either entrance and climb the stairs carefully to sit in one of the 400 seats, and enjoy the magnificence of the stage set. The acoustics are remarkable –there are no microphones or artificial amplification used in performances. The theatre is still used for concerts and other events, and there is a small shop at the entrance that can provide booklets and more information.

Teatro Olimpico is such a treasure that it's worth spending time there exploring the entrances that provide some information about the history including the first performance. The translation of this poster in the entrance hall puts this place in perspective. 'On March 3, 1585, thus, in the world's most famous theatre, the world's most excellent tragedy is performed.'

Ready for a Pick-me-Up?

Checking out this beautiful renaissance theatre can be tiring. If you're in need of a break, there are several cafes adjacent to the Piazza Matteotti that may be very comfortable. If you're in the mood for lunch in a fabulous 'emporium' as well as restaurant, you're in luck.

Il Ceppo is practically next door to Palazzo Chiericati at Corso Palladio 196. It was jammed with diners and shoppers each time I walked by but, if you have the time, the crowds indicate that it's worth the wait. Even if you don't want to wait, it's worth going in and perusing the shelves of gorgeous Italian products and beautiful displays of luscious food. It may be just the place for those delicious Italian edible souvenirs.

Pinacoteca Civica di Palazzo Chiericati

Hours: Tuesday–Sunday, 9:00A.M.–5:00P.M.
Closed on Monday
July–August, 10:00A.M.–6:00P.M.
Price: € 15,00 or included in the
Biglietto Unico Museum Card.

Pinacoteca Civica di Palazzo Chiericati is the Civic Museum for the city of Vicenza.

Palazzo Chiericati is a gorgeous Renaissance palace that Palladio designed in 1550 for Girolamo Chiericati, one of the Vicentian leaders during the period. Palladio also designed a private villa for the Chiericati family in the countryside outside Vicenza.

It's interesting to note that the beautiful Piazza Matteotti was once the cattle market for the city of Vicenza. Oh, how times have changed. Take a moment to admire the exterior of this beautiful building. The statuary on the roof, the columns, the loggia, and the large windows are all hallmarks of Palladio's genius.

The Palazzo was acquired by the City of Vicenza from the Chiericati family in 1839. The museum first opened in 1855. The city has been restoring it for many years.

When I first visited the Palazzo in 2010, I could only access the first floor.

If you've chosen to purchase the Biglietto Unico or Museum Card, you can walk right in by showing the card to the guard at the entrance.

As you enter the Sala del Firmamento, the first main room, look up at the extraordinary ceiling fresco *(pg 23)*.

This beautiful fresco was the work of Domenico Riccio della Brusasorzi, a Renaissance painter from Verona. This is a stunning fresco depicting Apollo, in a fascinating and somewhat provocative view, racing a chariot across the sky. The fresco was completed in 1558 and is titled "Phaeton Driving the Chariot of the Sun."

Surrounding the main fresco are smaller emblems including zodiac figures and other symbols. It's worth spending time looking at the wondrous ceiling.

There are some explanation panels on the walls that are helpful and can provide more information.

As you move into the museum, enter the Sala dei Lunettoni (the Hall of the Civic Lunettes). This hall contains a group of paintings consisting of seven large lunettes portraying the governing leaders (or Mayors) of Vicenza, who were called Podestas, by celebrated painters of the time, Jacopo Bassano, Francesco Maffei and Giulio Carpioni.

These lunettes illustrating each Podesta are remarkable and fascinating to study for the way they depict the Vicentian civic leaders. A wonderful example is the lunette of Podesta Alvise Foscarini seen below.

This painting by Francesco Maffei glorifies Podesta Foscarini, shown with one of his two sons. The background includes references to Venezia, the capital of the Veneto, and Foscarini's father who was a military leader. The Foscarinis were a wealthy and influential Venetian family during the Renaissance. The family also had Palladio build a villa on the Brenta Canal. We'll visit the Brenta Canal in Walking Tour #8 although we won't visit this particular villa.

Each lunette has an information pedestal in English and Italian that provides more details about the painting and the history at the time.

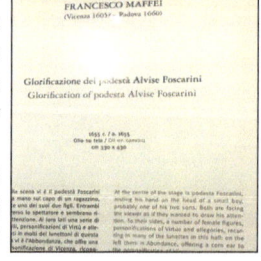

Some historians suggest that the 16th century during which Vicenza was under

Vicenza Teatro Olimpico and Palazzo Chiericati

Venetian control was the city's 'golden age.' The Podestas who governed Vicenza during this period were able to bring a degree of stability to the area that, in turn, encouraged such artists as Palladio to flourish.

This painting by Francesco Maffai next to the entrance to the gallery represents the golden age of Vicenza. It depicts St. Vincent holding a golden model of the medieval city of Vicenza. If you look carefully, you can see Palladio's Basilica in the model.

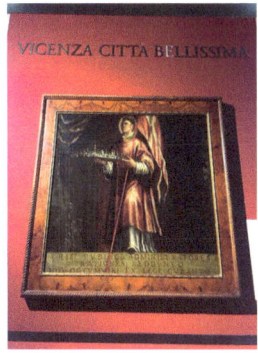

This museum's paintings and art objects highlight the notion of Vicenza's golden age as you progress up to the other floors.

The first floor has paintings from the medieval period with masterpieces by Montagna and Veneziano.

One painting that I particularly liked is The Madonna of the Stars by Marcello Fogolino.

In the background it depicts Vicenza with Palladio's Basilica and the clock tower in Piazza dei Signori.

Fogolino was one of the local painters who were influential in increasing the prominence of Vicenza's community of Renaissance artists.

This painting by Bartolomeo Montagna depicts the Madonna between the Saints Monica and Mary Magdalene. Montagna was also very influential in raising the stature of Vicenza's artists during the Renaissance. You can also see the city of Vicenza in the background of this painting. The face of St. Monica on the left is reputed to be a portrait of Piera Porto, a 15th century aristocrat in Vicenza who is believed to have commissioned the painting in memory of her late husband.

Moving up to the Second floor, you'll find galleries containing Venetian 15th century masterpieces by Bassano, Tintoretto and Veronese, among others. Take a leisurely wander through the galleries enjoying these paintings.

In one of the galleries on the second floor, you'll find these extraordinary terrestrial and celestial globes. This pair was made in 1640 by master cartographers in Amsterdam. They are fascinating to look at and give

Vicenza Teatro Olimpico and Palazzo Chiericati

you a view into what was known in the heavens and on the earth at that time. They also have fascinating symbols. There are similar globes in the Doge's Palace in Venezia but here you can take your time examining them without crowds and, unlike in Venezia, you can photograph them like I did.

There is also an example of a "Caravaggisti" or "tenebrosi," as followers of Caravaggio were called. Caravaggio was a baroque master from Rome and the subject of a prior book. Imagine my surprise at finding this painting in the 17th century collection.

This painting is called 'the Palm Reader' or 'The Fortune Teller' and was painted by Pietro Della Vecchia in about 1650. Caravaggio painted numerous 'Fortune Tellers,' one of which is in the Louvre in Paris, and another in the Museo Capitolini (Capitoline Museum) in Rome. Caravaggio was an acknowledged master of the style of chiaroscuro, or dramatic lighting. Notice how Della Vecchia's painting illustrates this technique with the diagonal shadow from left to right.

Do not miss the Attic!

The top floor or Attic of the museum has a number of contemporary pieces, which is quite surprising. The Attic houses the collection of Guiseppe Roi, an Italian marquis who left his books, papers, paintings, and other materials to the Civic Museum. The rooms are set up as though you are in the library and sitting rooms of a private home. The paintings include wonderful items such as this charcoal by John Singer Sargent.

Another treasure I found was this beautiful watercolor by French Impressionist Jean-Baptiste Camille Corot.

You'll also find some fascinating photographs of the Marquis with such luminaries as Princess Margaret. It's clear to me that the Marquis led quite a life

Vicenza Teatro Olimpico and Palazzo Chiericati

After spending several hours in this jewel of a museum, head back along Corso Palladio until you arrive at Piazza dei Signori for a well-deserved break.

Ready for a Pick-me-Up?

Museum visits can be exhilarating as well as exhausting. As you cross the piazza, head back toward the Basilica. If you need a break, consider returning to the same café I recommended in Walking Tour #1.

There are other places but Garibaldi's is my favorite. It is a gorgeous place for a break and allows you to sit and sip your prosecco or an Aperol spritzer with a full view of the Basilica and all the happenings in the piazza. On a sunny day, there are few more delightful places to relax and enjoy this part of Italy.

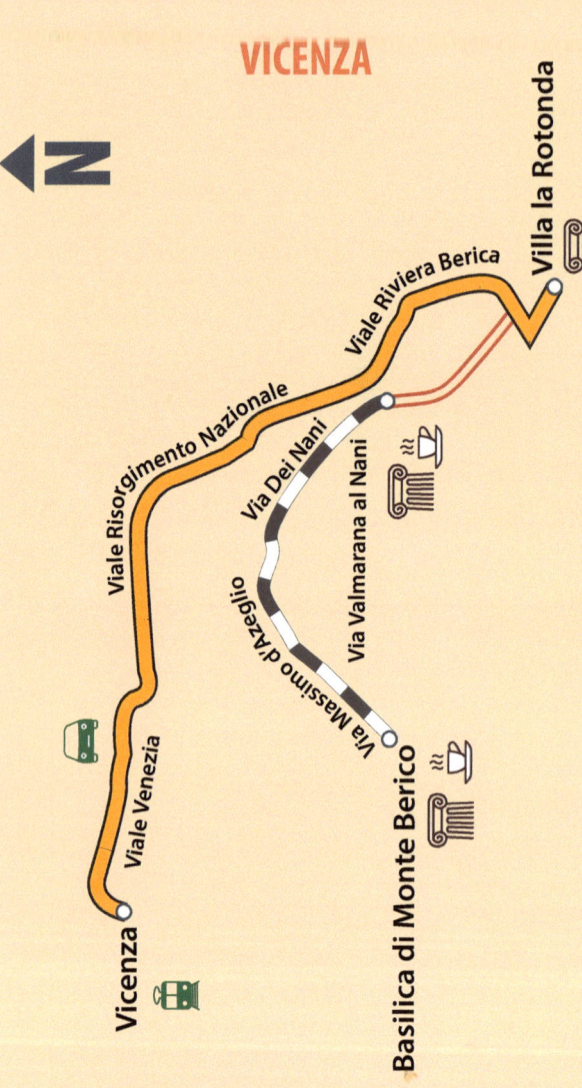

Walking Tour #3
Villa Rotonda, and Villa Valmarana ai Nani

Walking tour #3 starts at the Vicenza train station located at the intersection of Viale Venezia and Viale Roma.

If you don't want to drive to La Rotonda, you can also take a #8 bus from the Vicenza railway Train Station, or hire a taxi. From the train station, a taxi ride to La Rotonda is approximately € 10.

If you're driving, know that La Rotonda is only 3 kilometers from the train station. Follow Viale Venezia away from the station and bear right onto Viale Risorgimento Nazionale. After less than one kilometer, bear right onto Borgo Berga and follow it, as it becomes Viale Riviera Berica. After approximately one kilometer, turn a slight right onto Via della Rotonda and follow it up the hill around to Villa La Rotonda on the left. There is on-street parking only so it's best to arrive in the morning and park along the road. Pay attention to the signs. The website for Villa La Rotonda also notes that there is parking at the Benza petrol station in Viale Riviera Berica.

http://www.villalarotonda.it/en/visiting.htm

Villa la Rotonda

Hours: March 10–November 10, (except on Monday), 10:00A.M.–12:00P.M., 3:00p.m.–6:00P.M.
November–March, 10:00A.M.–12:00P.M., 2:30–5:00P.M.
Interior Visits: allowed only on Wednesday and Saturday. **Price:** € 10,00
Exterior Visits: Sunday, Tuesday, Thursday, Friday.
Price: € 5,00

Villa la Rotonda is one of most significant achievements of Andrea Palladio. According to the official website, German author J.W. Goethe, upon visiting for the first time, noted: *"Maybe never architectural art has reached such a level of magnificence."*

The Villa is also known as Almerico-Capra villa, and was designed by Palladio in 1570. It has four facades and is stunningly beautiful from every angle.

The design was also inspired by the Pantheon in Rome and the dome was originally conceived with an oculus or opening in the middle of the dome.

Paolo Almerico, a retired priest who was originally from Vicenza, commissioned the villa. He retired from a religious career at the Vatican and the interior of the building still retains some religious imagery.

The villa was ceded to the Capra family in 1591. It was ultimately purchased by the Valmarana family, a noteworthy aristocratic family from the Veneto, who restored La Rotonda and opened it to the public in 1986.

The last member of the family/owner of the villa was Mario di Valmarana who died in 2010. Interestingly, Valmarana served for a time as a professor of architecture at the University of Virginia (UVA). During his tenure at UVA, Valmarana founded the university's study-abroad programs in Vicenza and Venezia.

Presumably, Valmarana came to UVA because of the university's connection to Palladio. Thomas Jefferson designed his beloved home Monticello based on Palladio's writings and drawings about La Rotonda in his books *I Quattro Libri dell'Architettura* (The Four Books of Architecture). In fact, Jefferson took the name 'Monticello' (little hill in Italian) from Palladio's descriptions of La Rotonda.

Although Palladio designed the villa and began the construction of it, he died in 1580 before it was completed. As noted in the prior walking tours, Vincenzo Scamozzi, another prominent architect, was actually the one who finished the building. Scamozzi wanted the dome to have the oculus and be open to the sky. Apparently rational minds prevailed as La Rotonda's dome was completely covered with a cupola at the top.

If possible, you should plan to visit on a Wednesday or a Saturday so you can walk through the interior of the villa. I was able to visit the interior and it's beautiful as well as very comfortable. There are four main sitting rooms around the circular area beneath the dome. The interior originally was designed without bedrooms but now there are circular staircases to the upper level with bedrooms in each corner. A balcony runs around the interior of the dome. Spend some time looking at the sitting rooms, the beautiful fireplaces and the frescoes in the interior.

Do not ignore the exterior with its gardens and walkways. When you walk around the exterior, you'll get to see each of the four beautiful facades and the views on all sides. The city of Vicenza is visible from one of the sides.

There is also a beautiful book and gift shop located in the outbuilding adjacent to the entrance gate and staircase up from Via della Rotonda.

When you have finished at La Rotonda, you can walk to Villa Valmarana ai Nani by way of Via Valmarana, a private path that takes about 8 minutes to walk.

Walk back down the entrance steps to Via della Rotonda and turn right. On the other side of the road, you'll see a sign directing you to the path. Turn left and follow the path. The path is easy to follow but is a bit rocky so I suggest wearing flat heeled walking shoes.

It's a beautiful walk and you will arrive at Via dei Nani and the entrance gates to the villa on the left.

Villa Valmarana ai Nani

Hours: March–November; Open every day from 10:00A.M.–6:00P.M.
Price: € 10,00

Ready for a Pick-me-Up?

After arriving at the Villa Valmarana ai Nani via the beautiful walking path, you may be ready for a break. You're in luck! This villa comes with a charming café. Il Caffe di Villa Valmarana is part of the guest house (Foresteria) of the Villa.

>Hours: Monday—Wednesday and Friday,
>11:00A.M.—2:00P.M and 4:00-6:00P.M.
>Thursday, 11:00A.M.—2:00P.M.
>Saturday and Sunday, 11:00A.M.—6:00P.M.

There is a beautiful outdoor terrace and indoor seating with a Tiepolo gracing the walls.

This beautiful villa was not designed by Palladio, but is reminiscent of his style and, as a close neighbor to La Rotonda, it should not be missed. It was built in about 1670.

Villa Valmarana ai Nani means 'villa of the dwarves.' The legend about the house is that the daughter of the villa's first owner was a dwarf princess and servants, who were also dwarves, surrounded her. According to the legend, she took her own life when she came to the realization about her differences. The 17 dwarf statues on the wall outside the villa were originally scattered about the gardens; then moved to the wall at a later date.

The Villa is famous for its frescoes by Giambattista Tiepolo and his son Giandomenico. Tiepolo was a prominent artist from Venezia and he painted the cycle of frescoes in approximately 1757.

These amazing frescoes depict mythological and literary events from the Iliad, the Aeneid and Homer, among others.

The fresco on the previous page is in the room dedicated to Homer and depicts 'Eurybates and Talthybios Lead Briseis to Agamemmon.'

This fresco is in a room that is based on the Liberated Jerusalem, which was considered one of the greatest heroic poems by Torquato Tasso, an Italian poet and playwright who lived in the 17th century.

These frescoes are simply stunning and worth examining closely. They are full of wonderful detail such as this beautiful little dog in the corner of one of the paintings.

Both times I've visited this villa, I've been able to spend time contemplating these beautiful paintings without huge crowds.

In addition to being the home of these glorious and celebrated frescoes, Villa Valmarana ai Nani is still the home of the Valmarani family. Family photographs and other small treasures decorate the beautiful furniture in each of the rooms. In one room, I discovered this charming photograph of the head of the family with the Queen 'Mum' of England.

In still another room, I learned about the villa's partial destruction by an allied bomb in World War II, as evidenced by this photograph that showed the main salon just as they were beginning reconstruction.

This is a magical place to leisurely wander through and you get a sense of how the Italian aristocracy actually lived.

There is also a wonderful book and gift shop on the lower level of the Villa and, if you have the time, you can watch a short film about the Villa and the family for an additional charge. The staff in the Book Shop call this the Immersive Room and

the charge is € 2,50 for a 7-minute-video, € 4 for an 11-minute video.

Do not ignore the gardens. Wander outside and stroll through the beautiful paths through the various sections of the park. The photograph below shows one of the views from the park in which you can see the Sanctuary of Monte Berico in the distance.

At the end of your visit, there is another bookshop in the Forestia, adjacent to the Café, along with a wonderful portrait of Palladio.

You can return to your car by using the same path as you took to get to the Villa from La Rotonda or you can continue to another treasure just outside Vicenza, the Sanctuary of Monte Berico.

If You Have the Time

If you have additional time, Basilica di S. Maria di Monte Berico (Sanctuary of Mt Berico) is a beautiful basilica just outside Vicenza. The church is atop a hill overlooking Vicenza and Mt. Grappa. You can drive to the basilica or you can walk to it from Villa Valmarana.

To walk, leave the Villa Valmarana and turn left onto Via dei Nani, the road next to the wall lined with stone dwarves. Continue uphill in the same direction along the walled, cobbled Via San Bastian. You will reach a leafy hillside street with benches, Via Massimo d'Azeglio. At the end is Viale 10 Giugno, which climbs up to the Basilica di Monte Berico.

To drive, return to your car parked at Villa Rotonda. Drive back down the hill of Via Rotonda and bear left onto Viale Risorgimento Nazionale. Turn left at Viale Dante Alighieri and follow it up the hill to Viale 10 Giugno and the basilica is on your left. There is a small parking area at the Piazzale della Vittoria, the plaza in front of the church.

Either driving or walking is a reasonably short distance of approximately 10 minutes.

> Hours: Daily, 6:00A.M.–12:30P.M. AND 2:30P.M.–6:00P.M.
> Saturday and Sunday, 6:00A.M.–6:00P.M.

The Basilica was built in the 15th century, according to legend, after the townspeople of Vicenza prayed to St. Mary to rid them of the plague, and she directed the people to build a church. The Vicentians built the church in three months; and the plague apparently died out shortly thereafter.

The church was remodeled multiple times and it is said that Palladio did some design work there. On a sunny day, the vista from Monte Berico is beautiful.

On clear days, you can even see the foothills of the Dolomites.

The interior of the church is sumptuously baroque. There are paintings by Veronese and by Mantegna.

When you've finished, there are also several cafes nearby to enjoy before you return to Vicenza.

VERONA

- Galleria d'Arte Moderna
- Piazza dei Signori
- Piazza della Erbe
- Arche Scalig and Arena
- Torre dei Lambe
- Casa di Guilett
- Via G Mazzini
- Arena Piazza Bra
- Corso Porta Bosari
- Parcheggio Cittadella
- Corso Porta Nuova
- Stazione Verona Porta Nuova

Walking Tour #4

Walking Tour #4

Verona Highlights

Verona is the second largest city in the Veneto, anchoring the western end of the province just as Venezia anchors the east.

There was a settlement here since before Roman times and so much history and romance that it's a must-see place in any tour of the Veneto. Shakespeare set two of his most popular plays in Verona and, to many, Shakespeare established Verona as a major tourist destination by locating the tragic romance of 'Romeo and Juliet,' and the comedy of 'Two Gentlemen of Verona' here, even though there is no evidence that Shakespeare himself ever traveled to Verona.

In 2000, the city of Verona was named a UNESCO World Heritage site because of its historical preservation of urban structures and architecture from 2,000 years of uninterrupted development[4].

Verona Card

In this walking tour and walking tour #5, we will visit some sights that require an entrance fee. The Verona Card is available for tourists and covers a variety of museums, churches and galleries. You can buy the Verona Card in the monuments, and museums and in the IAT Tourist Information Office. An IAT office is located in Piazza Bra. These are some of the attractions that are covered under the Verona Card:

- **Torre dei Lamberti**
- **Casa di Giulietta**
- **Castelvecchio Museum**

---

[4] UNESCO World Heritage Sites, including the World Heritage List

- San Zeno Basilica (Walking Tour #5)
- Arena at Piazza Bra (Walking Tour #5)

Prices: € 18,00 for 24 hours
€ 22,00 for 48 hours

In this walking tour, we will visit Piazza della Erbe, Piazza dei Signori, Casa di Giulietta (Juliet's Balcony), and Palazzo della Torre. We will end with a side tour of the nearby town of Soave, for those of you with a car.

Walking tour #4 starts at the Stazione Verona Porto Nuova (Verona train station) located at the Piazzale XXV Aprile. Or, if you are driving, I suggest parking at a parking garage near Piazza Bra, such as Parcheggio Cittadella.

The parking garage is on Via Marcantonio Bentegodi, 8, roughly a 4 minute drive from the station, if there is no traffic. Verona is a challenging city to drive in so be aware that you're better off walking.

To walk from the train station: Note: this walk will take approximately 25-30 minutes so you may want to consider taking a taxi instead.

Head east on Piazzale XXV Aprile Turn left to stay on Piazzale XXV Aprile. Turn left at Piazzale Venticinque Aprile Turn right onto Piazzale Venticinque Aprile. Continue onto Via Statale 12. Turn left onto Piazzale Porta Nuova. Continue onto Corso Porta Nuova. Continue onto Piazza Bra and walk past it (Piazza Bra will be covered in Walking Tour #5).

Note: To walk from a parking garage near Piazza Bra: this walk from the parking garage will take approximately 13 minutes.

Leave the Parcheggio Cittadella and turn left onto Piazza Cittadella. Walk around the Piazza until you reach Corso Porta Nuova and turn right onto Corso Porta Nuova.

Continue onto Piazza Bra but, if you can, walk past it. We'll spend time in Piazza Bra in Walking Tour #5.

Continue onto Via Dietro Anfiteatro. Turn left onto Via Giuseppe Mazzini, a gorgeous street lined with shops, cafes and hotels. Stay on Via Giuseppe Mazzini until you reach Via Cappello. Turn right and continue a short while until you arrive at Piazza della Erbe.

Piazza della Erbe

Piazza della Erbe is Verona's historic market square or forum, and its enormous space is surrounded by art galleries, cafes, restaurants and historic buildings. It's the heart of Verona and simply cannot be missed.

At one end of the Piazza is the Colonna di San Marco, shown above. This column has a marble version of St. Mark's Lion at the top. This is the symbol of Venezia, as Verona was under Venetian rule for several centuries.

In the middle of the Piazza is the fountain that holds an ancient statue known as the Madonna of Verona. The statue is Roman and dates from 380 AD.

At the other end of the piazza is another column erected in the 14th century and bas-reliefs of Mary, St. Zeno, the patron saint of Verona, and other saints.

Piazza della Erbe is always bustling. Take some time and walk through the stalls. You never know what you'll find amongst the 'treasures,' souvenirs and knick-knacks. The vendors are friendly and fun to talk with.

Ready For a Pick-me-Up

Piazza delle Erbe is the center of Verona and tourists, students and the Veronese are always here enjoying 'la dolce vita'. Depending on the time of day, you'll find plenty of cafes serving caffe, Aperol Spritzers, snacks and lunches. Pick one that suits you and enjoy the ambience!

When you're ready to move on, walk back over to Via Cappella passing Torre dei Lamberti and take a look. This is Verona's tallest tower. It was built by the Lamberti family, originally in the 12th century and restored in the 15th century after lightning struck the tower damaging the top of it. The tower is 278 feet high. The tower has two bells named the Rengo and the Marangona respectively. Both bells were central to keeping time in Verona and sounding the alarm for fire and other emergencies. The bells supposedly are currently rung during funerals.

Verona Highlights

> **If You Have the Time**
>
> You can visit the inside of Torre dei Lamberti, if you wish. You go up in the tower either by a set of stairs or by elevator. The views at the top are panoramic. The view of the city from this tower is spectacular.
>
> Hours: Daily, 10:00a.m.–7:00p.m..
> Price: € 6,00 or included with the Verona Card

Continue on Piazza delle Erbe until you reach Via della Costa. Turn left and walk to the next Piazza.

This is Piazza dei Signori, a beautiful airy plaza with a magnificent statue of Dante Alighieri in the middle.

The piazza is also called 'Piazza Dante' in honor of the statue. Dante lived in Verona for several years after he was banished from Florence in 1312. The statue was erected in 1865. It is believed that Dante lived in one of the buildings lining this piazza.

Palazzo della Rangione is adjacent to Piazza dei Signori. This stunning striped building with a magnificent Gothic staircase dates from the 12th century, and since 2014 is home to the Galleria d'Arte Moderna Achille Forti, or Gallery of Modern Art.

> ### If You Have the Time
>
> If you are interested in visiting the Galleria d'Arte Moderna Achille Forti museum, the entrance fee is included if you purchased a ticket to Torre dei Lamberti.
>
> Hours: Tuesday–Friday, 10:00A.M.–6:00P.M.
> Saturday and Sunday, 11:00A.M.–7:00P.M.
> Closed on Monday
> Price: € 4,00 or included with the Verona Card.

As you walk past Piazza dei Signori, continue on Via Santa Maria Antica to the far corner of the Piazza. There you'll find the Arche Scaligeri, or the tombs of members of the Scaligeri family who ruled Verona in the 13th and 14th centuries.

These tombs are incredibly ornate. You can't do more than just look at them from the outside but they are worth it. They are considered great—if a bit 'over the top'—examples of Gothic art.

When you've finished with the tombs and Piazza dei Signori, retrace your steps back to Piazza Erbe and turn right on Via Cappella. Continue heading down Via Cappella until you reach #23. Look left and enter the courtyard. This is the courtyard of Casa di Giulietta. You can't miss this because it's likely to be crowded with hordes of tourists wanting a view of 'Juliet's Balcony' and to touch the breast of the statue of Juliet for good luck.

When you visit, you'll notice that Juliet's breast is extremely shiny due to the multitude of tourists wanting to have good luck! The building is from the Renaissance period but there is no evidence that Juliet or any member of the 'Capulet' family lived here, despite what the signs proclaim. In fact, the balcony wasn't added until sometime in the 20th century. And the statue was put in the courtyard in the 1970s. Still it's a must-see to visit in Verona.

If You Have the Time

If you are interested in visiting Casa di Giulietta, you can tour the house, and stand on the balcony. You can tour multiple rooms and see the costumes from the Romeo and Juliet movie released in 1968 and directed by Franco Zeffirelli.

Hours: Tuesday-Sunday 8:30A.M.–7:30P.M.
Monday 12:30–7:30P.M.
Price: € 6,00 or included with the Verona Card.

Our last stop on this walking tour is a view of the remains of Palazzo della Torre, the only Palladian building in Verona.

Leave the courtyard of Casa di Giullietta and turn left on Via Cappello. Turn left onto Via Giuseppe Mazzini and follow it to the next block. Turn right onto Via Quattro Spade and walk up the next block. Turn left onto Corso Porta Borsari. Palazzo della Torre is just off the Corso di Porta Borsari, at #27. Turn left and walk into the courtyard at Padovano, 3, Vicolo Cieco Fondachetto.

Inside the block sits the remains of Palazzo Della Torre (also known as 'Dalla Torre'). It was designed by Palladio for Giambattista Della Torre, who was a friend of some of Palladio's patrons. The building was probably designed around 1555 but was never finished, and was heavily damaged by World War II bombs.

Architects and scholars know about the building because of Palladio's drawings of it in his books on architecture, *I Quattro Libri dell'Architettura*.

To return to your parking garage or to the train station, return to Corso Porta Borsari and turn left. Continue a few blocks and turn left onto Via Valerio Catullo.

Turn right onto Via Giuseppe Mazzini and continue retracing your steps back to Piazza Bra and the Arena.

Turn right onto Via Dietro Anfiteatro and you'll see the Arena and Piazza Bra ahead of you.

Ready for a Pick-me-Up?

There are wonderful outdoor restaurants and cafes that line the perimeter of Piazza Bra. I was refreshed at Liston 12, a charming outdoor cafe with a beautiful view of the arena.

Find one with an open seat, signal the waitperson, relax and enjoy the circus! You'll probably notice around you that, at any time of day, a very popular drink is an Aperol Spritzer, or glass of Prosecco. After all the walking, go ahead and enjoy one. You deserve it!

Walking Tour #5

Verona's Basilica—San Zeno Maggiore with the Mantegna altarpiece and Piazza Bra

Walking Tour #5 starts at the Stazione Verona Porto Nuova (Verona train station) located at the Piazzale XXV Aprile. Or, if you are driving, I suggest parking at a parking garage near Piazza Bra, such as Parcheggio Cittadella, which is roughly a 4-minute drive from the station, if there is no traffic. Verona is a challenging city to drive in so be aware that you're better off walking.

Verona is such a wonderful place to visit but many visitors do not venture beyond the Piazza Erbe and Piazza dei Signori. As wonderful as they are, and we visited those in Walking Tour #4, however, the Basilica of San Zeno is worthy of an extended visit. San Zeno Maggiore is a masterpiece. It is one of the best preserved Romanesque churches in Northern Italy. It was also considered to be a model for other churches of the same period.

To walk from the train station, leave the Piazzale XXV Aprile and head in the direction of the Adige River on Via Citta de Nimes. Bear left onto Piazza Renato Simoni. Continue onto Via Giovanni della Casa. Continue onto Via Carmelitani Scalzi and shortly make a slight right onto Stradone Porta Palio. This is about a 20-minute walk. Ahead of you is a beautiful castle structure known as Castelvecchio.

To walk from a parking garage near Piazza Bra, leave the Parcheggio Cittadella and turn left onto Piazza Cittadella. Walk around the Piazza until you reach Corso Porta Nuova and turn right onto Corso Porta Nuova. Turn left onto Vicolo Volto S. Luca and continue onto Piazza Arditi. Head toward Castelvecchio that you can see in the distance. Turn right onto Via Daniele Manin and keep walking until you reach Castelvecchio. It's about a 20 minute walk.

As you reach the Castelvecchio, turn left and climb the stairs. Follow the walkway next to the Adige River, Largo Don Bosco. You're next to Regaste San Zeno. This ancient walkway gives you gorgeous views of the Adige River. Follow the Largo until you reach the stairs. Climb down the stairs and do a slight right onto Via Barbarani Berto. Turn left onto Piazza Corrubbio and follow the Piazza around to the right. Through the trees, you'll see Piazza San Zeno and the Basilica on the right at one end of the piazza. Stop for a moment and just take it in.

Verona's Basilica—San Zeno Maggiore

This is a remarkable building that's been serving the religious needs of the people of Verona since the 12th century.

It is named for San Zeno, the patron saint of Verona. San Zeno was the eighth bishop of Verona and was appointed about AD 350. His tomb is located in the Crypt. San Zeno was credited with converting Verona to Christianity.

The adjacent campanile or bell tower has been there as long as the Basilica. The bell tower was constructed over a long period between 1045 and 1178. Both the church and tower were constructed of Italian tufa stone and bricks. To me, it's amazing that this edifice is still standing and in use. There's actually been some kind of a church on this site since the 7th century.

As you approach the entrance, you'll see a pair of ancient lions holding up columns that flank the door. Apparently they are named 'Justice' and 'Faith.' Also notice the wealth of marble bas-relief carved panels on the front of the church. The panels portray Old Testament stories. Also the enormous Rose window above the door was created in the early 13th century.

The entrance to the church is along the left side of the building.

San Zeno Basilica

Hours: Monday–Saturday, 8:30A.M.–6:00P.M.
Sunday, 12:30–6:00P.M.
March–October:
10:00P.M.–1:00P.M. & 1:30–5:00P.M.
Monday–Saturday, 12:30p.m.–5:00P.M.
Price: € 2,50 or included with the Verona Card.

As you enter, you'll see the cloister, a beautiful peaceful space complete with both Romanesque and Gothic arches. The cloister is all that's left of a 13th century Benedictine Abbey that was destroyed during the Napoleonic Wars.

As you enter the basilica, the crypt is on the left and the main altar is on the right.

Verona's Basilica—San Zeno Maggiore

The Basilica is most famous for its three-part altarpiece or triptych by Veronese master Andrea Mantegna in 1457. The altarpiece is incredibly beautiful and is considered one of the first Renaissance masterpieces in the Verona area. It's a stunning depiction of the Virgin and child and served as an inspiration to many artists of the area.

As beautiful as the triptych is, you're seeing a copy because the original was stolen by Napoleon and never returned to Italy. It is now the property of the Louvre in Paris. However, the copy that you see here is still full of beautiful details like the two garlands above the Virgin Mary. The frame is the original one and is actually attributed to Mantegna himself. It's interesting that Napoleon left it behind.

As you wander around the nave of this basilica, notice the ancient frescoes.

The frescoes were painted by various artists during the 14-15th century and some are scenes of San Zeno's life. What I found fascinating was the 'graffiti' etched on the frescoes supposedly by the monks who lived and worked at the basilica in times past. Take a closer look at them. Some are dated; for example, '1390' and '1862.' I find it amazing that they apparently were allowed to do that!

This beautiful fresco above the prior one depicts St. George and the Princess by an unknown Veronese artist. This was painted in the 13-14th century and is in remarkable condition.

Another masterpiece to study is the set of carved bronze doors. The artists are unknown but the doors contain 48 carved panels

Verona's Basilica—San Zeno Maggiore

depicting scenes from the Old and New Testament and are very well preserved. These doors are believed to have been constructed in the 11th century.

Also worthy of a look is a polychrome statue of San Zeno from the 13th century. The saint is depicted as smiling, which is very unusual and interesting.

You must also visit the Crypt, if for no other reason than it's supposedly the place where Shakespeare's Romeo and Juliet were married. The Crypt also holds the tomb of San Zeno.

Spend some time in this beautiful basilica. In addition to the treasures and the history, San Zeno serves as a great respite from the tourist throngs that can invade Verona.

When you leave San Zeno, retrace your steps and walk along the Adige River, enjoying the scenery along the way and the views of the Ponte Scaligero, the bridge that is part of the Castelvecchio.

As you reach Castelvecchio, climb down the stairs and follow the road around it.

If You Have The Time

Take a moment to reflect on this beautifully restored medieval fortification. Castelvecchio was built in the 13th century on what was probably the site of an ancient Roman fortress.

Castelvecchio is what many would envision if they were asked what a medieval castle would look like.

It's a mammoth structure complete with seven towers, battlements and crenellated walls on the side of the Adige River. The remains of a moat that was fed by the river surround it. Castelvecchio is now a Museum of the City of Verona and hold Veronese arts from many periods, historic artifacts and ecclesiastical art objects.

Hours: Daily 8:30a.m.–7:30p.m.;
Monday 1:30–7:30p.m.
Price: € 6,00 or included in the Verona Card

As you reach the street leading to Ponte Scaligero, you'll cross over onto Corso Castelvecchio. Turn left onto Corso Castelvecchio and turn right onto Via Roma. Via Roma is a beautiful main street that will lead you to Piazza Bra.

Verona's Basilica—San Zeno Maggiore

> **Need a Pick-me-up?**
>
> If you want to hang out near the Castelvecchio, consider one of the charming cafes along Via Roma. One that has gotten great reviews is Via Roma 33 Café that will also give you great views of the castle. The café is a charming, and is open for breakfast or a caffe after visiting the Castelvecchio.

Piazza Bra and the Arena

Piazza Bra is the largest piazza in Verona and is a must-see for visitors. The Piazza is surrounded by cafes and beautiful buildings including the world-famous Arena, a Roman amphitheatre built in about AD 30, making it almost 2,000 years old.

The Arena is built of pink and white limestone and has been stunningly restored and maintained, both inside and out. It is now a renowned music venue with opera and contemporary music performances.

The Arena di Verona Festival operates a summer program of operas inside the Arena, and can accommodate over 20,000 concertgoers. It is famous for its large-scale productions, such as Aida that features live elephants on stage. The festival operates from June through September.

https://www.arena.it/arena/en

The Arena was also the site for several movies including the gladiator scenes in the 2000 movie 'Gladiator' starring Russell Crowe.

If you are interested in a walking tour of the Arena, the Arena is open every day.

    Hours: Tuesday–Sunday, 8:30a.m.–7:30p.m.
            Monday, 1:30p.m.–7:30p.m.
    Price: € 10,00 or included in the Verona Card.

Verona's town hall, the Palazzo Barbieri, is also adjacent to Piazza Bra. The neoclassical Palazzo is Verona's City Hall and was built in the 19th century by architect Giuseppe Barbieri. It has been the headquarters for Verona's government since 1869.

The Gran Guardia is the other primary government building on the Piazza. The original structure was begun in the early 17th century to shelter soldiers. In 1808, Barbieri, the same architect for Palazzo Barbieri,

Verona's Basilica—San Zeno Maggiore

designed the current building. It is a magnificent structure, using many elements that are using many elements that are emblematic of Palladio's signature designs.

The other grand buildings include the palaces surrounding the Piazza that were built in 16-17th centuries for members of Verona's aristocracy.

The statue in the middle of the park is that of Victor Emmanuele II, the first ruler of united Italy. It was erected in 1883.

Piazza Bra is a wonderful place that is one of the hearts of the city of Verona. While it is frequently crowded with tourists, it's still a great place to sit and contemplate the throngs, the Arena and the ambience while sipping a Prosecco or an aperitif such as an Aperol Spritzer.

Ready for a Pick-me-Up?

There are wonderful outdoor restaurants and cafes that line the perimeter of Piazza Bra. I was refreshed at Liston 12, a charming outdoor cafe with a beautiful view of the arena.

Find one with an open seat, signal the waitperson, relax and enjoy the circus! You'll probably notice around you that, at any time of day, a very popular drink is an Aperol Spritzer, or glass of Prosecco. After all the walking, go ahead and enjoy one. You deserve it!

After relaxing in one of the most beautiful piazzas in Italy, return to your car in the nearby parcheggio, or to the train station. It's been a busy day!

PADOVA

Walking Tour #6

Walking Tour # 6

Padova (Padua) the Home of The Scrovegni Chapel with Giotto's Frescoes

Padova (Padua) is the actual birthplace of Palladio. While he was born here, Palladio has no existing villas or other buildings in Padova.

So, while we won't see any Palladian villas, we will see some spectacular historic buildings and artifacts. Padova is one of the most interesting cities in Northern Italy. Padova is also the setting for part of Shakespeare's "Taming of the Shrew." As mentioned in Walking Tour #4, Shakespeare set another of his most famous plays in the Veneto even though there is no evidence that he ever visited Italy. However, Padova is so historically and visually rich, it is a must-see on a visit to the Veneto. To that end, for our first walking tour in Padova, we are visiting a world-famous masterpiece, The Scrovegni Chapel, home of the Renaissance painter Giotto's masterwork.

Walking Tour #6 starts at the Padova Treni Stazione, the central train station in Padova, located at Piazzale Stazione. Padova is a challenging city to drive into so I strongly recommend that, if you're driving, you find a parking garage near the train station. There are several parking garages nearby that are identified with a large blue **P**.

Padova Card

As I mentioned in other walking tours, several cities in the Veneto have tourist cards that enable visitors to easily access numerous sites within the city, including the Scrovegni Chapel. In addition to the Chapel, other sites covered by the Padova Card include:

- The Eremitani Civic Museums
- Palazzo della Ragione
- Piano Nobile Cafè Pedrocchi
- Museum of the Risorgimento
- Reduced ticket to Orto Botanico

The good news about the Padova Card is that you can use it for public transportation—the tram or the bus to get around inside Padova.

The Padova Card is valid 48 or 72 hours from the starting date stamped on it.

Price: 48-hour card: € 16,00
72-hour card: € 21,00

You can buy the Padova Card at the train station and you can also make timed reservations for the Scrovegni Chapel there as well.

You can also make reservations online if that's your preference.

A site I've used and found reliable is SelectItaly.

https://selectitaly.com/tickets/museums/the-scrovegni-chapel/244

Or, you can also now book online directly with The Scrovegni Chapel

http://www.cappelladegliscrovegni.it/index.php/en/

A reservation is strongly recommended. When I visited in October, I was only able to make the reservation for the next day but fortunately I had planned on several days in Padova.

To walk to Scrovegni Chapel, leave the train station and turn left on Piazzale Stazione heading toward Via Daniele Donghi. Turn left onto Corso del Popolo and keep walking. This is one of Padova's main streets. After you cross the Via Trieste, the street you're on becomes Corso Guiseppe Garibaldi.

Padova (Padua) the Home of The Scrovegni Chapel

Continue on Corso Giuseppe Garibaldi. As you walk, you'll notice a beautiful park on your left. This is the Park Giardini dell'Arena, the site of an ancient Roman arena. Continue to walk around the perimeter of the Park onto Piazza Eremitani and continue a short way until you see the signs for the chapel on your left.

This is approximately an 8-minute walk.

Scrovegni Chapel

Hours: 9:00 A.M.–7:00 P.M., year round;
each visit is limited to 15 minutes
Price: € 10,00 or included in the Padova Card.

Plan to arrive at the Chapel well ahead of your timed reservation. The building houses a terrific book and gift shop as well as restrooms. Take a few minutes to wander around the bookstore and the colonnade, which is actually part of the Eremitani Museum complex. This is a very beautiful place with some interesting antiquities such as this fragment of ornate frieze so linger if you can.

That said, the Scrovegni Chapel is the main event here.

The Scrovegni Chapel is a masterpiece, known throughout Italy and Europe as the height of Giotto di Bondone's or Giotto's art. Giotto was a renowned late-Middle Ages/early Renaissance painter who came from Florence. The Scrovegni Chapel was constructed in about 1305 and it is said that Giotto and the artists from his workshop completed the frescoes in two years. The frescoes depict scenes from the life of the Virgin Mary and the life of Jesus Christ. The back wall of the chapel contains the world famous fresco of Giotto's Last Judgment. Many scholars believe that these frescoes herald the beginning of the Renaissance. By the way, Giotto was 38 years old when he completed these frescoes!

Enrico Scrovegni, a wealthy banker in Padova, commissioned the chapel. It was originally planned as a larger church with room for the tombs of Enrico and his wife. The Scovegni Palace was originally at the site and was to be connected to the chapel. In addition, at the time of the chapel's construction, the Eremitani church apparently complained that Scrovegni's church had the potential to overshadow their existing complex so the Padovan leaders ordered it scaled back. The Scrovegni palace was torn down in 1827 and, incredibly, the chapel

Padova (Padua) the Home of The Scrovegni Chapel

was almost destroyed at that time as well. It also suffered damage in World War II but has been painstakingly restored so we can all enjoy and appreciate Giotto's genius.

It is also said that Enrico Scrovegni had the chapel erected to atone for his father Reginaldo being mentioned by name as a usurer in Dante Alighieri's *Inferno*, part one of his 14th century epic, *The Divine Comedy*. The timing of the chapel's construction and the publication of Dante's Inferno don't really work but there are symbols within the chapel that lend credence to the tale anyway.

Plan to get to the ticket office at the chapel at least 15 minutes before your reserved time on the tickets. There is a security check so be prepared. A tour guide will direct you to the waiting room, which is outside the chapel. Always carry your tickets with you, as they will be checked.

Do not be late. The signage and the website include warnings that late visitors will not be admitted.

Each group of visitors has a maximum of 25 individuals admitted at a time. When the access doors open automatically and you walk in, you'll be ushered into a waiting room for 15 minutes. Be aware that the entrance doors open only once. Once seated, you'll be shown an interesting film with English (and other languages) sub-titles that outlines the history and the extensive restoration of the chapel and the frescoes.

The film gives you a good overview and helps set context. However, the real purpose of the time in the waiting room is to help stabilize the climate in the chapel.

Those of you who have visited DaVinci's 'The Last Supper' in Santa Maria della Grazie in Milan will have experienced a similar 'climate-control' process.

After 15 minutes, automatic doors will open and you will be able to enter the chapel. Your visit there is limited to 15 minutes, unfortunately way too short a time to thoroughly explore this magnificent structure.

When you enter, you'll walk in and turn right on the aisle to face the fresco of 'The Last Judgment.'

The beauty of the chapel as well as the extraordinary quality of the restoration immediately struck me. The colors are remarkable as well as breathtaking. The small size of each visitors' group means that you'll really be able to see and photograph the frescoes, although without a flash. They are so amazing that, for me, it was a bit hard to take in.

If you didn't realize it before, you might recognize some famous elements in the frescoes. For me, the most recognizable figure was that of the devil in the lower right section of 'The Last Judgment.' I'm not sure in what art book I first saw this gruesome image but I certainly never forgot it.

Padova (Padua) the Home of The Scrovegni Chapel   71

The devil is depicted as chewing on a poor naked soul who was condemned to the Inferno. The figure is surrounded by others writhing in agony at their endless damnation. And that's a river of red blood pouring down onto the damned souls from the Christ figure seated in the middle.

When you think about the early 14th century, relatively few individuals were able to read or write so the wealth of illustrations around the chapel, such as this one, definitely underscored the church's teachings about the implications of heaven and hell.

Although 'The Last Judgment' is, for me, the highlight of the visit, please take some time to look at the incredible array of scenes from the Bible. They represent notable stories from the Old and New Testament, life of Mary and scenes from the life of Christ. Giotto actually painted them to represent scenes that are in chronological order horizontally. However, when you also look at each set of panels vertically, they represent variations on similar themes.

Pictured on the left are three frescoed panels. The middle panel depicts the Raising of Lazarus and the lower panel represents Christ's Resurrection. Both are 'resurrections.'

Here's another panel. The middle fresco represents the Entry of Christ into Jerusalem while the lower panel depicts the Ascension of Christ into heaven, both representing the entry of Christ into a new place.

One of Giotto's most famous frescoes in this chapel is on the opposite wall.

The lower panel depicts the betrayal of Christ by Judas Iscariot in the Garden of Gethsemane. Giotto's version depicts Jesus and Judas staring at each other while Judas kisses him, very powerful imagery indeed. The soldiers who arrest Jesus and the disciples who are trying to protect him are also depicted. St. Peter is shown on the left stabbing a soldier with a knife.

As you wander about the thirteen sepia toned images of

These are fascinating figures. They are monochromatic in trompe d'oeil relief. On the right is the image of the Vice 'Envy.' Notice the snake coming from the woman's mouth and biting her on the nose.

She's also 'burning with envy,' perhaps the origin of that famous phrase.

The second image is that of the Vice 'Despair.' It's terrifically sad with the poor woman figure hanging from a noose.

The other set of images are the Virtues. This one depicts the Virtue of Charity. The woman in this image has a large bowl of fruit that she is distributing. In one hand, she is depicted as giving a large pear to an angel, illustrating her qualities of serenity and generosity.

Before leaving the chapel, take a closer look at The Last Judgment again. On the lower left side near the center of the fresco is a depiction of Enrico Scrovegni himself. He is illustrated offering the Scrovegni Chapel to the figures of Hope, Charity and Faith, or possibly St. Mary. This is considered a realistic portrait of Scrovegni. Interestingly and perhaps wishful thinking on Giotto's or his patron's part, Scrovegni is also depicted as one of the 'resurrected' souls.

However generous and charitable Scrovegni was, at some point he fell out of favor with Padova's leaders and he left the city to live in Venezia where he died in 1336. He was buried in this magnificent chapel.

Also take note of the stunning star-studded ceiling. Giotto painted images of saints and prophets among the stars in the ceiling. You can still see the rich blue color and the whole effect is simply beautiful. By the way, when I was there, the Gift Shop had really pretty pocket-sized screen/phone cleaners decorated with the  image of this ceiling. And if you by chance needed a pocket square for your blazer pocket, it can serve as that too.

It's disappointing that you only have 15 minutes to view these magnificent frescoes. It's almost too much to take in. But the automatic doors open again and you are ushered out of the chapel en masse, while the next group of visitors awaits.

Padova (Padua) the Home of The Scrovegni Chapel

If you have the time after this compressed tour, wander through the books and gifts in the Gift Shop. They have wonderful, reasonably priced souvenirs and gifts. I found I appreciated the wares more after seeing the Chapel than I did before I entered.

> ### Ready for a Pick-Me-Up?
>
> Although the Scrovegni Chapel tour is not that long, you may need a break. The perfect place in Padova is the famous Pedrocchi Café. The Pedrocchi has been a central meeting point for everyone who's anyone in Padova for well over a century and its reputation is well-deserved. This is not only a fabulous café, but it is also a must-visit stop on any visit to Padova.

It's a relatively short 7-minute walk to Pedrocchi Café.

When you leave the Scrovegni Chapel, turn left and head back to Corso Giuseppe Garibaldi. Turn right on Garibaldi and continue walking on Corso Giuseppe Garibaldi.

You will reach Piazza Garibaldi and walk across it to Via Cavour. Continue onto Via Cavour and you will reach Piazza Cavour. Continue onto Via VIII Febbraio and Pedrocchi's will be on the right.

Pedrocchi Café

Via VIII Febbraio, 15m

The interiors of Pedrocchi are sumptuous and elegant. Experienced waiters encourage you to linger and enjoy your surroundings. They are also very knowledgeable; the ones I had were delighted to tell you about the history if they were not too busy.

If nothing else, order the Caffe Pedrocchi, a minty-green coffee drink that is really more of a rich dessert. It comes with chocolate dipping cookies too.

There is also an adjacent bakery with luscious French macaroons and a variety of mouth-watering pastries.

When you've finished your lunch or afternoon snack, you can also tour the Piano Nobile Caffè Pedrocchi, the upstairs rooms that are decorated in Moorish, Egyptian, and Greek themes and contain all manner of artifacts from Padovan history. Access to these rooms is included in the Padova Card.

Padova (Padua) the Home of The Scrovegni Chapel

The photo on the left shows the ceiling of the Greek room.

In the mid-19th century, Pedrocchi's became the center for the 'Risorgimento' movement. This was a group of students who met to strive for Italy's unification and independence from Austria. There are fascinating materials in the rooms that commemorate that time, such as this poster dated February 10. During one of these events in February 1848, students led an uprising and several were executed.

If the weather is good enough and the doors are open, you can even step out on the balcony and look out on Via VIII Febbraio.

Continue to relax at Pedrocchi or return to your hotel to savor and contemplate the wondrous things you've seen today.

PADOVA

- Padova Treni Stazione
- Corso del Popolo
- Scrovegni Chapel
- Piazza Eremitani
- Corso Garibaldi
- Piazza dei Signori
- Pedrocchi Café
- Piazza delle Erbe
- Riviera Tito Livio
- Piazza del Santo
- Basilica di Sant' Antonio
- Orto Botanico
- Prato della Valle

Walking Tour #7

Walking Tour #7

Highlights of Padova

This walking tour will take in some of the other sights of Padova including the beautiful Piazza dei Signori, Piazza della Erbe, the magnificent Basilica di Sant' Antonio, and the famous Orto Botanico, the first major Botanical Garden in Europe and the world.

Walking Tour #7 starts at the Padova Treni Stazione, the central train station in Padova, located at Piazzale Stazione. Padova is a challenging city to drive into so I strongly recommend that, if you're driving, you find a parking garage near the train station. There are several nearby that are clearly marked with a large blue **P.**

Padova Card

As I mentioned in other walking tours, several cities in the Veneto have tourist cards that enable visitors to easily access numerous sites within the city, including the Scrovegni Chapel. In addition to the Chapel, other sites covered by the Padova Card include:

- The Eremitani Civic Museums
- Palazzo della Ragione
- Piano Nobile Cafe Pedrocchi
- Museum of the Risorgimento
- Reduced ticket to Orto Botanico

The good news about the Padova Card is that you can use it for public transportation—the tram or the bus to get around inside Padova.

The Padova Card is valid 48 or 72 hours from the starting date stamped on it.

Price: 48-hour card: € 16,00
72-hour card: € 21,00

You can buy the Padova Card at the train station and you can also make timed reservations for the Scrovegni Chapel there as well.

Leave the train station and turn left on Piazzale Stazione heading toward Via Daniele Donghi. Turn left onto Corso del Popolo and keep walking. This is one of Padova's main streets. After you cross the Via Trieste, the street you're on becomes Corso Guiseppe Garibaldi.

Continue on Corso Guiseppe Garibaldi. As you walk, you'll notice a beautiful park on your left. This is the Park Giardini dell'Arena, the site of an ancient Roman arena.

You will reach Piazza Garibaldi and walk across it to Via Cavour. Continue onto Via Cavour and you will reach Piazza Cavour. Continue onto Via VIII Febbraio and Pedrocchis will be on the right.

The Pedrocchi Café is open every day and has been the meeting place of scholars, artists, writers and everyone who's anyone in Padova. It was opened in 1831 by Antonio Pedrocchi and is a wonderful fixture in Padovan life. There is indoor and outdoor seating and I encourage you to try both venues, as this is a place for multiple visits when you're in Padova.

You can stop at Café Pedrocchi or continue, remembering that this is a must-stop on your way back.

Head south on Via VIII Febbraio toward Via Guglielmo Oberdan through Piazza dei Frutti to Piazza dei Signori.

Piazza de Signori

Piazza dei Signori is one of the major squares in Padova. It is a very pretty piazza surrounded by arched walkways, shops and cafes and, at the end the Palazzo del Capitanio, constructed in the early 16th century for the militia. The Palazzo is known for its tower with an astronomical clock. In front of the Palazzo is an ancient

Roman column holding the symbol of Venezia, the Lion of St. Mark.

Adjacent to the Capitanio is a beautiful building known as Loggia della Gran Guardia. This Renaissance building was erected in the late 15th century as a government building and was used for the militia during the Austrian occupation.

Retrace your steps back through the piazza. Turn right onto Via Municipio and walk over to Piazza delle Erbe.

Piazza delle Erbe

Piazza delle Erbe is one of the largest piazzas and is frequently filled with market stalls selling all kinds of items. This is considered one of the largest open-air markets in Italy.

The major sight here is the Palazzo della Ragione, or 'The Palace of Reason.' This was the medieval court of justice. Although the loggia on the Palazzo has been unofficially attributed to Palladio, there is no proof of that. However, the building looks remarkably similar to Palladio's Basilica in the center of Vicenza so this could be a striking copy.

The interior of the Palazzo is filled with frescoes and worth seeing if the building is open. There is also an enormous wooden statue of a horse that was constructed in 1466 and apparently paraded around the piazza by a team of oxen.

Spend some time in the beautiful Piazza delle Erbe.

Moving on to the Basilica di Sant' Antonio, head east on Piazza delle Erbe toward Via Fabbri. Continue onto Via Fiume and Piazza della Frutta. As you head toward Riviera Tito Livio by way of Via Guglielmo Oberdan and Via Cesare Battisti, you will pass by the Universita degli Padova, or one of the main halls of the University of Padova. The University is the second oldest in Europe and Galileo was actually a professor there! As you explore Padova, you'll see University buildings in many sections, as well as references to Galileo.

Keep walking onto Via S. Canziano and onto Via S. Francesco. Turn right onto Riviera Tito Livio and walk down this street. This street also has trams so, if you wish, using your Padova card, you can take a tram from the Tito Livio stop to the Santo stop.

If you decide to keep walking, turn left onto Via Gaspara Stampa and walk to Via del Santo and then to the Piazza del Santo.

The Basilica is right on the piazza. This is about a 10-minute walk.

Highlights of Padova

The Basilica of St. Anthony

Hours: Daily, 6:20 A.M.–7:45 P.M.

This enormous church was built in the 13th century to honor St. Antonio, the patron saint of Padova. Although St. Antonio was reputedly a simple but powerful preacher, the city of Padova went a bit overboard building such a lavish structure to house his tomb. It is reminiscent of St. Mark's in Venezia.

While the exterior seems almost Byzantine, the interiors are richly decorated and are a combination of Romanesque, Gothic, Renaissance and even a bit Baroque in style. Wander around and admire the sumptuous marble decoration and bas-reliefs.

And notice the pilgrims. St. Antonio's Basilica is a very popular pilgrimage site as it is one of eight shrines designated by the Vatican. One source said that over 5 million pilgrims visit St. Antonio every year.

The central nave is really beautiful and full of copious decoration. St. Antonio's tongue is housed in a reliquary in the nave—quite a big deal in pre-renaissance times. The early Renaissance master Donatello sculpted six statues of saints in the high altar as well the enormous crucifix.

Also worthy of your attention are the marble bas-reliefs depicting the miracles of St. Antonio. They are really stunning and a careful examination reveals beautiful details.

This relief depicts the miracle in which St. Antonio reattaches the foot of a young man. It was sculpted by Antonio Lombardo in the 16th century.

There are a lot of beautiful artifacts inside the various chapels including one that I never found. Apparently, there is a funeral monument of Luigi Visconti inside the Basilica that is attributed to Palladio but this is not proven. I actually didn't find the monument but you're welcome to look for it.

As you leave the Basilica, take care to notice the beautiful equestrian statue in the Piazza del Santo, in front of the Basilica.

This statue is considered the earliest surviving Renaissance equestrian statue and was very influential in inspiring other sculptors of equestrian monuments. If you've been to the Capitoline Museum in Rome, this is reminiscent of the statue of Marcus Aurelius in that museum. This statue was created by Donatello in 1453 to commemorate a Venetian military officer named Erasmo da Narni, who was also known as "Gattamelata."

There's one last stop on this walking tour; the beautiful Orto Botanico di Padova or the Botanical Garden of the University of Padova. This garden was founded in 1545 and was listed as a UNESCO World Heritage Site in 1997. This is the oldest botanical garden in the world and contains an important collection of rare plants that was created by the Faculty of Medicine at the University.

The good news is that it's right around the corner from St. Antonio and Donatello's statue.

Head south on Piazza del Santo toward Via Orto Botanico Turn left onto Via Orto Botanico and walk toward the sign that you can see next to the gate for the garden.

Orto Botanico di Padova

Hours: April–September, 9:00 A.M.–7:00 P.M. (every day; closed on working Mondays).
In October, the gardens close one hour earlier at 6:00 P.M.
During the winter months, November–March, the gardens close at 5:00 P.M.
Price: € 10.00, € 5.00 with the Padova Card.

The gardens are really extraordinary, especially given their age. UNESCO, when citing them as a World Heritage Site, noted:

"The Botanical Garden of Padova is the original of all botanical gardens throughout the world, and represents the birth of science, of scientific exchanges, and understanding of the relationship between nature and culture. It has made a profound contribution to the development of many modern scientific disciplines, notably botany, medicine, chemistry, ecology and pharmacy."[5]

The gardens retain elements of their original design, the oldest part being a circle divided into four quarters and surrounded by a wall. The garden originally was called a 'Garden of Simples,' and contained 2,000 medicinal plants. Its purpose was to enable the students to study herbal medicines and be able to distinguish actual medicinal plants from false or dangerous ones. The garden now contains over 6,000 plants.

As you walk through the garden, you'll see an incredible array of plants including some ancient ones. Sections are marked and individual plants are identified by their Latin or scientific names. Wander through the gardens and prepare to be amazed. Be on the lookout for an ancient palm known as Goethe's Palm or St. Peter's Palm. It was planted in 1585!

The aquatic pools contain a thriving array of water lilies and other plants that are sustained due to a constant temperature from an ancient artesian well.

Be prepared to linger in this wonderful place for a while. There is also a well-stocked gift shop with clean restrooms in the Entrance building.

---

[5] United Nations World Heritage Centre http://whc.unesco.org/en/list/824

If You have the Time

Prato della Valle is a huge piazza (actually in an oval shape) that has been a significant part of Padova since Roman times. It is located adjacent to Orto Botanico and is yet another beautiful site in Padova. It's a 5-minute walk from the Botanical Gardens.

At 90,000 meters, it is the largest piazza in Italy.

To get there, leave the main building at the Orto Botanico, and head back to Via Orto Botanico. Follow the road until you reach Via Donatello. Stay on Via Donatella until you reach the roadway next to Prato della Valle. Turn into the piazza and spend some time admiring its symmetry and beautiful statuary.

There are 78 statues in the inner and outer ring, all by various artists. There were originally 88 statues, but some were destroyed by Napoleon in 1797. They represent famous figures in Padovan and Italian history and are known as the 'illustrious Persons.' A statue of Gallileo is included somewhere in the array. See if you can find it!

This piazza began as a Roman arena; then was a cattle market; then it was neglected until it became a swamp. The piazza was resurrected by the Venetian government in 1767 and became the beautiful plaza that you see today.

> ### Need a Pick-me-up?
>
> By this time, you may need a rest and some refreshment after all this walking. There are multiple cafes and restaurants surrounding Prato della Valle. Just pick one and enjoy an Aperol Spritzer or prosecco, and watch the people and beautiful piazza.

When you're ready to finish this walking tour, you can take the Padova Tram back to the train station or retrace your steps. To walk, head to the north end of Prato della Valle and follow the roads back to Corso Giuseppe Garibaldi and the train station. It's about a 30-minute walk.

Or you can take the tram. The Santo tram stop is next to the Sant'Antonio Piazza, and the Prato Valle stop is just outside Prato della Valle. Remember, the cost of the tram ride is included in your Padova card, and the trams are fun to ride and pretty efficient. Trains usually run about every 10-15 minutes and the ride to the Piazzale Stazione is approximately 15 minutes.

Enjoy your return to your hotel after a very full day.

BRENTA CANAL

Walking Tour #8

Walking Tour #8
Padova to Venezia—Cruising on the Brenta Canal

This walking tour is partly walking and partly an 8-hour boat ride that will deliver you past voluptuous summer palaces that belonged to wealthy Venetians, ultimately dropping you at the famous Piazza San Marco in Venezia. It's an incredible experience and one that was a highlight of my trip to the Veneto! And you'll get to visit one of Palladio's most famous villas.

Padova Card

As I mentioned in other walking tours, several cities in the Veneto have tourist cards that enable visitors to easily access numerous sites within the city, including the Scrovegni Chapel. In addition to the Chapel, other sites covered by the Padova Card include:

- The Eremitani Civic Museums
- Palazzo della Ragione
- Piano Nobile Caffè Pedrocchi
- Museum of the Risorgimento
- Reduced ticket to Orto Botanico

The good news about the Padova Card is that you can use it for public transportation—the tram or the bus to get around inside Padova. That is why I've included mention of it in this walking tour.

The Padova Card is valid 48 or 72 hours from the starting date stamped on it.

Price: 48-hour card: € 16,00
72-hour card: € 21,00

You can buy the Padova Card at the train station.

The tour company is called Burchiello Tours. http://www.ilburchiello.it/en/tour

They run tours both ways between Padova and Venezia. Tours run from March through October. In 2017, the price for one adult was € 99,00, expensive but, in my opinion, worth it. You can also pay ahead for a lunch at a restaurant on the canal about half way through the tour. I purchased tickets online ahead of time at their site and found that it worked well.

Walking Tour #8 starts at the Padova Treni Stazione, the central train station in Padova, located at Piazzale Stazione. Padova is a challenging city to drive into so I strongly recommend that, if you're driving, you find a parking garage near the train station. There are several nearby that are clearly marked with a large blue P.

The tour starts at the **Portello Gate,** the old river port where the tour boat is docked.

To reach the port, you can walk but you can also take a bus, especially easy if you have purchased the Padova Card. To take the bus, exit the Train Station and walk across the street to the bus stop (Ferrovia-Catasto) at the Piazzale Stazione. Look for bus #07 and travel down the Via Tommasseo, going three stops to the Tommaseo 114 stop. This is next to one of the entrances to the University of Padova. Turn right on Via Venezia and walk approximately two minutes to reach the river. The Portello Gate is across the street and you'll see the tour boat and a sign. The tour leaves at 8AM so be prepared to be there by about 7:30AM. There is a café right next to Portello Gate so you can purchase a cappuccino or caffe latte prior to boarding.

Padova to Venezia—Cruising on the Brenta Canal

Portello Gate is an ancient stop with a beautiful staircase built in the 16th century. At one time, this was the main stop for the boats and barges that linked Padova and its surrounding areas with Venezia.

The boat seats about 30-40 people with indoor and outdoor seating. Be prepared for variable weather, depending on the season. When my trip began, we started with fog and a little drizzle but about an hour into the trip, the fog cleared and the weather was gloriously sunny.

Regardless of the weather, the beginning of this tour is beautiful as you glide by the old city walls of Padova.

Eventually you'll be away from Padova's density and start to see suburban landscapes. You'll also see your first lock. The trip to Venezia travels through six locks and past numerous bridges, including some interesting 'swing' bridges.

I found it fascinating to watch the boat crew and the lock crews negotiate the locks. In one, they had to navigate around some quite sizeable debris but apparently that occurs fairly frequently on the cruise.

When the tour boat passes through the first lock, and you look through the eerie mist toward the poles and posts standing along the river, it's almost magical.

Padova to Venezia—Cruising on the Brenta Canal

Up ahead, you'll start to see the riverbanks and the beginnings of the Venetian summer villas.

The first stop is at Stra, Villa Pisani.

On my trip, the Villa magically appeared through the fog and mist and then we docked right in front of it.

The Villa is considered one of the most magnificent residences along the Brenta Canal. It was constructed in the early 18th century for the Venetian Doge Alvise Pisani, one of the noble families of Venezia during the height of its powers.

When the villa was completed in 1735, it actually had 114 rooms, to acknowledge that Doge Pisani was the 114th Doge of Venezia. The Villa had two architects; one from Padova named Girolamo Frigimelica, but the main building was ultimately completed by Francesco Maria Preti from nearby Treviso. They were both enamored

with neo-classico designs, which may be why the villa appears to be Palladian, or at least Palladian-inspired.

Villa Pisani has quite a history. As was the case with many Venetian patrician families, the Pisani family lost their fortune, in part due to gambling debts, and was forced to sell the Villa.

In 1807, Villa Pisani was purchased by the Emperor Napoleon! Napoleon purchased the villa during the short period of peace in Europe that was due to the Treaty of Tilsit. This occurred after France defeated Russia at the Battle of Friedland in July 1807. Peace, unfortunately, was short-lived and soon Napoleon was off on another campaign in the Iberian Peninsula. Napoleon's forces were ultimately defeated at Waterloo by combined forces of Britain, Austria, Germany and Russia in 1814.

In 1814 the Villa Pisani then became the property of the Hapsburgs of Austria who transformed the villa into a vacation villa for the European aristocracy of that period. Ultimately it was given to Italy as a public park.

In 1934 the Italian government restored Villa Pisani to enable Benito Mussolini to host his first meeting with Adolf Hitler.

As you walk through the Villa, you'll see some of the restored rooms with magnificent Baroque art and furnishings.

This Billiards room has a particularly beautiful set of frescoes.

You will also get to see Napoleon's bedroom, complete with his portrait. It's exceptionally grand with yellow striped silk on the walls and a gorgeous crystal chandelier.

The ornately draped bed has a sweet little Cupid at the top.

As you walk past Napoleon's bedroom, take a moment and note that he also had a richly decorated bathroom with a sunken bathtub.

Of all the rooms you'll visit, the most resplendent is the ballroom. It is two stories high and the ceiling was the last fresco that Giovanni Battista Tiepolo painted in Italy.

The painting on the ceiling is called The Glory of the Pisani Family, and was painted to honor the family. It's really stunning in its colors and perspective. Tiepolo's son, Giovanni Domenico Tiepolo, was also a painter and he assisted his father as well as painted some of the frescoes in other rooms.

During balls, the musicians would perform in the gallery above the ballroom floor. All in all, it must have been a splendid place for a party!

By the way, one of Tiepolo's little quirks, or perhaps amusements, was to paint some kind of little animal into the picture. In this ceiling, there is a parrot in the corner. See if you can spot it.

As you leave the Villa Pisani, make sure to walk through the sculpture gallery on the main floor. It's filled with beautiful classical figures in between the columns.

When you exit the villa, note the beautiful gardens and reflecting pools. The Villa Pisani is truly sumptuous and a reminder of the immense

Padova to Venezia—Cruising on the Brenta Canal

wealth of the Venetian nobility during the 15th–18th centuries.

Take one last view of the Villa Pisani as you reboard the Burchiello boat as well as the gorgeous surroundings along the banks of the Brenta Canal.

As you cruise along, you'll pass through several locks and swinging bridges that are fascinating to watch.

Eventually, the boat arrives at the country towns of Dolo and Mira, two towns along the canal where you'll start to see the highest concentration of magnificent Venetian villas along the banks.

In Mira, the second stop on the Brenta Canal tour is the Villa Widmann- Rezzonico- Foscari.

Villa Widmann-Foscari was built in 1719 during the period when wealthy Venetian families were constructing a considerable number of vacation villas. The Brenta River was considered cooler than the Venetian lagoon and gradually the popularity of summer villas in the Mira area became intensely competitive among the nobility and the families furnished their villas with almost-ostentatious adornments such as this extraordinary Venetian glass chandelier in the foyer.

The Villa Widmann-Foscari was also expensively embellished by extensive gardens with an array of beautiful cypress and horse-chestnut trees as well as stone statues of gods, nymphs and cupids.

The villa also has an extensive arcade adjacent to the gardens. The arcade, called a Barchessa, was used for storage and stables. With this villa, it was used to store the 'burchi', flat-bottomed riverboats, that the Venetians used to bring their household goods up the river to the villa. There is also a small church, where members of the Widmann family are buried.

All in all, these villas provide quite a picture of the ostentatious lifestyles of the Venetian nobility during the height of Venezia's influence, and there are stories of families starving themselves to maintain the façade of wealth.

Perhaps this competition was yet another contributing factor in the decline of Venezia as an economic power.

Returning to the Burchiello, you will continue along the Brenta passing some of the most beautiful countryside and magnificent villas side-by-side.

Reaching Oriago, the boat docks for lunch at Il Burchiello, a restaurant operated by the Burchiello Company. Lunch is extra and, while you don't have to purchase it, I saw no other options for dining.

After lunch and back on board, you'll pass through several more swing bridges on the Brenta.

The last stop is a visit to one of Palladio's most famous villas, the Villa Foscari, more commonly known as 'La Malcontenta.'

The villa was constructed for Nicolo and Luigi Foscari, members of a prominent Venetian family that also included a notable Doge. It was built between 1558 and 1560 based on Palladio's design.

The Foscari family used the villa for fancy receptions, and in 1574, the family most notably hosted King Henry III of France.

The name 'Malcontenta' is supposedly based on the story of a Foscari spouse who was confined there because of her disinterest in performing conjugal duties.

Look at the façade of the Villa Foscari that faces the Brenta. It looks remarkably like the front of La Rotonda, Palladio's famous villa in Vicenza. At one time, the villa had side wings but those were removed a long time ago. The rear façade of the villa overlooks beautiful gardens.

Padova to Venezia—Cruising on the Brenta Canal

The Foscari family owned the villa until 1797 when they abandoned it during the fall of the Venetian empire. The abandoned villa became derelict and decayed until the early 20th century when a wealthy South American family, the Landsburgs, purchased it and began a lengthy restoration process.

In 1973, Antonio Foscari (a descendant of the original Venetian family) purchased the villa, and undertook more of the restoration, bringing the villa back to its original grandeur. The family actually lived in the villa at times during the 20th century so the furnishings are more contemporary in design.

As seen here in this photograph, the family also undertook extensive restoration of the outdoor spaces and gardens. As you walk around the grounds, you'll also see another arcade, a Barchessa, was used for storage, stables, and 'burchi', flat-bottomed river boats,

You can also still see the small private canal that allowed the family to bring the boats up to the villa.

In 1996, La Malcontenta joined the other Palladian buildings as part of the UNESCO World Heritage designation.

Returning to the Burchiello boat again, you start the last part of the tour that ends in the Venetian lagoon.

This last part of the Brenta Canal tour is very different from the prior sections. You're getting closer to the Venetian Lagoon and you'll see more boats.

In this photo, an array of small motorboats lines the canal. You'll also pass through another lock.

Padova to Venezia—Cruising on the Brenta Canal

On the trip I took, we passed a gondola being launched, a very interesting process.

Suddenly, you're in the Venetian lagoon and I found that it's a magical sight. The Burchiello slowly enters the lagoon channel marked on both sides by channel markers.

It takes approximately 30 minutes to follow the channel across the lagoon to reach the Grand Canal.

Every minute is a photographer's dream! You first see an array of cruise ships and large private yachts. Then as you motor into the Grand Canal, you'll start to see the expected water taxis and gondolas traveling back and forth.

Then, all too soon, you're at the end of your eight-hour Burchiello tour and you disembark just beyond Piazza San Marco at the Ponte degli Schiavoni!

To see this at sunset is a miraculous sight and one I personally will never forget.

Padova to Venezia—Cruising on the Brenta Canal

Upon disembarking, you return to Padova by train from the Santa Lucia Stazione. You can reach the station by walking along the Grande Canal (approximately 30 minutes), or via a private water taxi, or by the Venezia waterbus. Any way you choose, it's all wonderful and gives you time to reflect on this extraordinary unique experience.

Ready for a Pick-me-Up?

If you have the time and want one more magical Venezia experience, you might consider Caffè Florian. Caffe Florian is the most famous and historic caffe in Venezia. It opened in 1720, making it reputedly the oldest café in the world according to Caffe Florian's website. It is located in Piazza San Marco underneath the arches of the Procuratie Nuove. It is quite expensive but the experience of sitting in Piazza San Marco, sipping a caffe, a Prosecco, or an Aperol Spritzer, and watching the world go by is quite remarkable.

BASSANO DEL GRAPPA

Walking Tour #9

Walking Tour #9

Bassano del Grappa and Palladio's Ponte degli Alpini and Asolo and Palladio's Villa Barbaro in Maser

This walking tour is a little different because, while there is a train station in Bassano del Grappa, I used a car to get there. I drove by car from Padova, a distance of approximately 50 kilometers or about an hour via main highways.

Both of these two towns are brilliantly beautiful and include magnificent Palladian masterpieces plus other incredible architecture.

Bassano del Grappa

In Bassano del Grappa, you will walk across what is arguably one of Palladio's and Italy's most famous structures, the Ponte Vecchio. In addition, you'll walk through one of Italy's most charming and historic towns.

Undoubtedly, the most famous and photographed site in Bassano del Grappa is the Ponte Vecchio (Old Bridge) also known as Ponte degli Alpini, or simply Palladio's bridge. The walking tour starts at the bridge.

Arriving by car

Driving in Bassano del Grappa is very challenging so I recommend that you park the car as soon as you can legally and walk.

Parking is unfortunately also a challenge. I was fortunate to be able to park on the street near Via Angarano on the western side of the town.

There is also a parking garage on Parcheggio Prato 1 located on Via Santa Caterina. If you park here, it's about a 9-minute walk to the Ponte degli Alpini. Leave the garage and head west toward Via Santa Caterina.

Turn left onto Via Santa Caterina and continue walking toward the Brenta River. Turn right onto Salita Gerhard Ott and shortly turn right onto Viale dei Martiri. Cross into Piazzetta Zaine and continue onto Vicolo Lazzaro Bonamigo. Turn left onto Via Lazzaro Bonamigo and then turn right onto Via B. Gamba. Follow Via Gamba to the Ponte Vecchio or Ponte degli Alpini.

Arriving by Train

If you arrive by train, the train station is located on Via de Blasi. You can take a train from Padova or Verona. If you arrive by train, leave the station and head north on Via de Blasi toward Via dell'Ospedale. You are heading west toward the Brenta River. It's about a twelve-minute walk to Ponte Vecchio.

Turn left onto Via dell'Ospedale. Cross Viale delle Fosse and walk down Via J. da Ponte. You'll reach one of the main piazzas of Bassano, Piazza Garibaldi. This is a wonderful piazza and we'll spend time there as part of this walking tour.

Keep walking toward the river and cross into the adjacent piazza, Piazza Libertà, another main piazza.

Cross Piazza Libertà and walk toward Piazzotto Montevecchio. Turn right onto Via Menarola and quickly turn left onto a small street called Salita Ferracina. This goes into Via Ferracina that parallels the Brenta River. Turn right and you'll see Ponte Vecchio in front of you.

Ponte Vecchio (Old Bridge) or Ponte degli Alpini

Palladio designed the Ponte degli Alpini, also known as the Ponte Vecchio, or old bridge, in 1569. It crosses the Brenta River. The bridge has been destroyed and rebuilt several times, most recently in 1948 at the end of World War II, when it was reconstructed according to Palladio's drawings. There are several stories about this last destruction—one is that the departing Nazis destroyed it; the second is that the town destroyed it to impair the German soldiers' ability to flee from the Allies. Whatever the true story is, the Alpini, the soldiers who fought in the Dolomiti, the Dolomite Mountains or the Italian Alps, returned to Bassano del Grappa, raised the money from private funds, and rebuilt this stunning bridge.

The Museo degli Alpini, the museum dedicated to the Alpine soldiers, sits at one end of the bridge and holds a number of artifacts about these soldiers. The museum is actually accessed through a bar so don't be put off by this. The displays include items donated over the years by locals and the alpine soldiers. It's a bit quirky but still interesting to see.

Hours: Tuesday–Sunday, 9:00 A.M.–8:00 P.M.

It is on the Argarano side of the Ponte degli Alpini bridge.

Walk across the bridge slowly taking in the magnificent views of the Brenta River and Mt. Grappa. This stunning view will bring you back many times. You will not be alone in admiring the beauty of this medieval town. During World War I, Ernest Hemingway billeted for a time in Bassano del Grappa while he served as an ambulance driver. F. Scott Fitzgerald and John Dos Passos also resided in Bassano during the World War I era.

Bassano del Grappa and Palladio's Ponte degli Alpini

At the other end of the bridge is the Poli Grappa Distillery with a showroom, retail shop and small museum including some artifacts of early Grappa distilling. It's well laid out and a great place for some Grappa souvenirs. Be aware that, during tourist season, the bridge can get very crowded in the afternoons and early evenings. There is a bar at each end and it's become popular to buy a glass of grappa at one end and sip it while walking to the other end to get another. Of course by the time you've sipped one small glass of grappa, your head—and everyone else's on the bridge—may be spinning. So consider how you want to spend your time here.

Once you've spent time admiring the bridge and view, head back toward the Piazzas that you passed by earlier. The streets are narrow and while some of them are pedestrian-only, you must pay attention and watch out for cars while you're enjoying the stroll. This is a real town inhabited by residents, not just tourists and the streets have shops, and small cafes designed to meet local needs. This is part of the charm of Bassano del Grappa.

Back in Piazza della Liberta, take a moment to view the square and enjoy its beauty, especially a beautiful building with a clock that is called the Loggia dei Podesta, or the Loggia of the Mayor.

This beautiful building was constructed in the 15th century to serve as the town hall. The clock was installed by Corrado da Feltre, apparently a clockmaker craftsman at the time, and added to the building in 1430. The southern side of the building also has a fresco of St. Christopher by Francesco Bassano il Vecchio, the father of Jacopo Ponti (known as Jacopo Bassano), a native son who became a famous 14th century painter.

Pass through this piazza to the adjacent Piazza Garibaldi, the second main square in Bassano. In one corner of the Piazza, you'll find the Museo Civico, the Civic Museum of the City of Bassano. The local Tourist Office is also located here.

Ready for a Pick-Me-Up?

Both Piazza Garibaldi and Piazza Liberta have multiple cafes with indoor and outdoor seating. Sitting outdoors in sunny weather is a wonderful opportunity to sip caffe, or an aperol spritzer, and watch the residents of Bassano stream by.

Museo Civico

Hours: 10:00A.M.–7:00P.M., every day except Tuesday.
Price: € 4,00

Bassano del Grappa opened this museum in 1831 in an old Franciscan monastery, and its collections include archeological artifacts, the history of the town and over 500 paintings of local favorite painter Jacopo Ponte (known as Jacopo Bassano). The museum also hosts special exhibits and I was fortunate to see one during my visit.

I saw a wonderful exhibit of Photographer Robert Capa's works. Robert Capa was a combat photographer whose photographs of the Spanish Civil War and the D-Day invasion, where he was the only civilian photographer on Omaha Beach, are world-famous. I'm not sure why the exhibition was in Bassano but I was lucky to see it.

If you parked your car in the Parcheggio Prato 1 located on Via Santa Caterina, you have one more sight to see in Bassano del Grappa. If you parked on the other side of Ponte Vecchio, I'd still suggest that you take a moment to view this sight.

Cross Piazza Garibaldi heading toward Torre Civica, the Civic Tower. Torre Civica was probably built about 1312 and it is possible to climb to the top of it if you're interested. You can see the tower in the photograph behind the Museo Civico. In fact, Torre Civico is a landmark that you can see from almost anywhere in Bassano del Grappa.

Leave Piazza Garibaldi and head up Via Vendramini toward Piazza Zaine. This is about a 4-minute walk up the hill. When you reach the Piazzetta Zaine, you'll have a beautiful view of the town. Turn right onto Viale dei Martiri and walk slowly down this beautiful tree-lined road. As peaceful as it seems now, this is a memorial of a bloody episode that took place here during World War II. Essentially members of the resistance were rounded up on Mt Grappa in September 1944, and 31 of them were hung from these trees. The avenue was renamed Viale dei Martiri, or Avenue of the Martyrs and each tree has a monument to the partisan who was murdered there.

Ready for a Pick-Me-Up?

At the intersection between Viale dei Martiri and Piazzetta Zaine is a locally-famous pastry and chocolate shop. Dolce Bassano is located at Piazzetta Zaine 14/15 and is filled with colorful handmade macaroons, luscious pastries and mouth-watering chocolates. Even if you don't have a sweet tooth, take a look at the beautiful displays of delectable sweets. I could not resist a few macaroons for the rest of my journey!

It's a sad and somber place while also being incredibly beautiful.

For such a small town, there is so much more to see in Bassano del Grappa. There is another villa designed by Palladio (Villa Angarano) on the other side of the bridge, and there is a museum dedicated to Ernest Hemingway and World War I, among other sites. I hope this has whetted your appetite for a longer visit.

The Villa Barbaro in Maser and the Village of Asolo

The second part of this 'walking' tour requires a car and some driving.

If you don't have a car, consider staying in Bassano and seeing more sites. As I noted earlier, the Tourist Office is located in Piazza Garibaldi.

However, if you do have a car or another means to get there, the Villa Barbaro in Maser is worth seeing as it is a magnificent Palladian masterpiece. It's considered by some to be Palladio's most striking villa, even more beautiful than Villa La Rotonda. It is also a UNESCO World Heritage Site.

Indeed, my first view of it was breathtaking!

To get there by car, leave Bassano del Grappa and look for signs for Maser and get on SP248. Essentially follow SP248 for about 23 kilometers and 35 minutes. You will pass through some charming villages and the scenery is pleasant. Your first view of Villa Barbaro will be from this road. Pass the Villa and follow the signs turning left on Via Barbaro. There is a parking area although it's not terribly large and is mostly grass.

Hours: April–October,
Tuesday–Saturday, 10:00A.M.–6:00P.M.
Sunday, 11:00A.M.– 6:00P.M.
Closed Monday
Price: € 9,00

The Villa Barbaro, also known as the Villa di Maser, was designed by Palladio and construction is estimated to have begun by 1560. The Barbaro family were among the leading patrician families in Venezia during the height of its power and influence. The family fortunes changed after Napoleon defeated the Venetians in May, 1797, and according to one source, the villa was eventually converted into apartments. The last of the family died in the mid-nineteenth century in impoverished circumstances. The villa continued to degrade and had multiple owners until 1934, when Count Guiseppe Volpi di Misurata, a wealthy Venetian banker and founder of the Venezia Film Festival acquired it and began the restoration. His descendants still live there today, which is why the touring is limited.

The Villa has six rooms that can be toured. They all have frescoes by the Venetian Renaissance artist Paolo Veronese that are quite striking. This fresco in the photograph is a trompe-l'œil delight, depicting one of the Villa Barbaro servants peeking around the door.

The villa is also known for its gardens, a collection of beautiful carriages and an out-building called a Nymphaeum, a structure that sat beside a natural spring that may have been used as a fishpond.

The villa is beautiful and gives you another glimpse into bygone Venetian aristocratic life. While access to the villa rooms is limited, you can wander about the grounds and admire the gardens. The villa

also produces its own wine and it is available for tasting and purchase in the shop that, in addition to wine, has local products, books and souvenirs for sale.

There is also a café where you can get a snack or a light lunch. For more information about the Villa and its facilities, the website is: https://villadimaser.it/en

However, I'd suggest a short drive to the beautiful hill town of Asolo. Asolo is the home of a justly famous hotel and restaurant, the Hotel Villa Cipriani. Asolo is about 10-12 minutes by car. Interestingly, the Villa Cipriani is also recommended by Villa di Maser, as it's listed on its website.

Return to your car, and head southeast on Via Barbaro toward Via Cornuda. You are essentially driving in the direction of Bassano del Grappa.

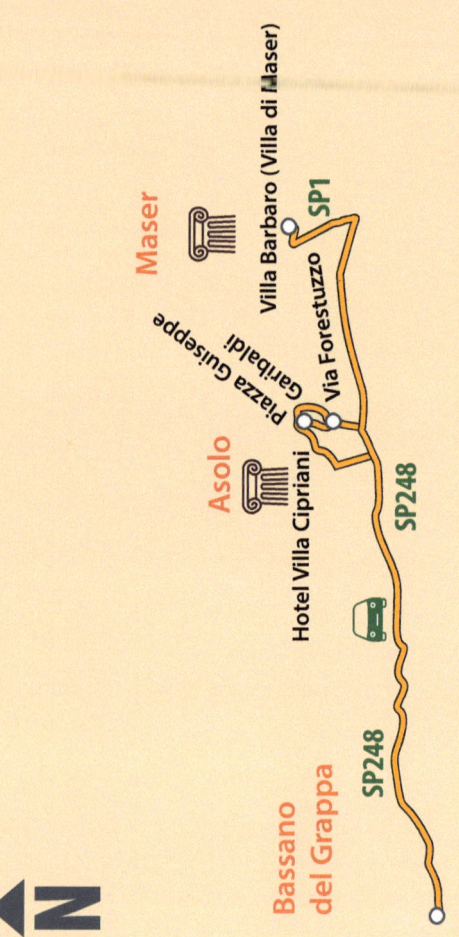

Bassano to Villa Barbaro and Asolo

Walking Tour #9a

Turn right onto Via Cornuda and continue onto Via Bassanese and SP 248.

After you pass through the village of Casella, watch for signs to Asolo and turn right onto Via Forestuzzo. You'll reach Asolo in about 1.5 kilometers.

Asolo

Asolo, located in the foothills of the Dolomites, is designated as a Borghi più Belli d'Italia, one of the most beautiful villages in Italy. It has been a mecca for intellectuals and artists since the 19th century. The poet Robert Browning, the novelist Henry James and Igor Stravinsky all lived there at various times. Asolo exudes an atmosphere of serenity and beautiful harmony; the name Asolo is actually derived from the Latin word Acelum that means 'sanctuary.'

There is a parking lot on Via Forestuzzo so leave your car and walk. It's an uphill walk but the views are worth it. Or, drive up the hill to the center of the town and take your chances of finding a parking space on the hilly streets.

The historical center of Asolo is Piazza Garibaldi, with its beautiful 16th century fountain. The town is beautifully maintained and is lined with charming shops, cafes and restaurants. Many of the streets are cobblestoned and 'pedestrian' only so you can walk without concern for cars. This is a place to wander, relax and enjoy the views around every corner.

Ready For a Pick-me-Up?

Honestly, in my opinion, one of the best reasons to visit Asolo is to have lunch at the Hotel Villa Cipriani. The Villa is a 'Palladian' era villa and so incorporates many of the features for which Palladio is renowned. The villa was purchased by the poet Robert Browning in 1889 and stayed in that family for several decades. In the 1960s, a member of the Guinness family purchased the hotel and modernized it while still keeping the charm and historic features intact. The manager of the Venezia Cipriani Hotel oversaw the renovation, which is probably how the hotel came to be part of that hotel group.

Lunch in the famous garden is a delight.

After a sumptuous and enjoyable lunch, walk around Asolo and locate the theatre dedicated to the actress Eleonora Duse. The theatre is located in a medieval building  known as the Castle of the Queen of Cyprus. Apparently, in 1498, Caterina Cornaro, the Queen of Cyprus, was ordered to leave Venezia and live in Asolo because of her interference in the politics of the Venetian Republic.

 Eleonora Duse was a famous Italian actress during the early 20th century. She owned a villa in Asolo and died there. The theatre was was restored in the 1930's and dedicated to the actress at that time.

The theatre is located within the historical center and has beautiful views of the valley below as well as Mt. Grappa and the Dolomites in the distance.

There are other sites to see in Asolo but perhaps the best thing about Asolo is that it's beautiful and you can simply enjoy it without being pressed to do anything.

When you're done with Asolo, return to your car and head for home.

VALDOBBIADENE and the PROSECCO WINE ROAD

Walking Tour #10

Walking Tour #10

Valdobbiadene and the Prosecco Wine Road

Valdobbiadene (pronounced Val-dough-BEE-AH-den-ay) may actually be the longest wine region name in existence. It is a spectacularly beautiful place and is the heart of the Prosecco wine appellation.

No tour of the Veneto region, in my opinion, is complete without a visit to the Prosecco region nestled in the foothills of the Dolomites. This region, under consideration for a UNESCO World Heritage designation, is dense with vineyards marching up the steep hillsides with the crags of the Dolomites hovering over them.

To get there, you must have a car but it's a relatively easy and beautiful drive from Bassano del Grappa or Vicenza.

> From Vicenza, head west on Via Galilei toward Via Niccolò Copernico and turn on to SP111 heading north west. At Cadore, you will reach the intersection with SP 248. Follow SP248 until you reach Bassano del Grappa. This drive is 17 km and should take only about 22 minutes.

> From Bassano del Grappa, look for signs for Maser and get or stay on SP248. Essentially follow SP248 for about 23 kilometers and 35 minutes. You will pass through some charming villages and the scenery is pleasant. Follow the signs and take SP 84 for Maser. You actually will be able to see Palladio's famous Villa Barbaro (Villa dei Maser) from this road.

> After you pass Villa Barbaro, continue on SP84 that is also known as Via Cornuda. Stay on SP84 until you reach the roundabout at Cornuda.

At the roundabout, take the 3rd exit onto SR348.
In 3.5 km, take the exit toward Cornuda/Vidor/Valdobbiadene.

At the roundabout, take the 2nd exit back onto SP 84 di Villa Barbaro/SP84.

You'll be crossing a bridge over the Piave River. At the roundabout, take the 2nd exit onto Via Erizzo/SP2.

Continue on Via Erizzo/SP2 to Viale Mazzini in Valdobbiadene.

The trip takes approximately 20 min (13 km) from Bassano and it's really stunning on a sunny day.

Piazza Marconi in Valdobbiadene is considered by some to be one of the prettiest piazzas in Northern Italy. The Piazza is anchored at one end by the Duomo di Santa Maria Assunta. There is parking along the streets leading into Piazza Marconi. Take a moment to walk up to the Duomo.

This cathedral was built in the 14th century but was updated to its current neoclassical style in the late 18th century. The beautiful bell tower with its onion dome is in the heart of the square, and dates back to the 17th century, but the steeple was added in 1810.

> ### Ready for a Pick-Me-Up?
> There are several cafes along the Piazza that are great places to stop and take a break. I enjoyed a delicious caffe at Café Roma, Piazza Marconi 14. I also saw many people enjoying Aperol Spritzers (made with Prosecco of course!) at 10 o'clock in the morning.

Just off Piazza Marconi is the Ufficio Informazioni Turistiche or Tourist Information Center. It is located at Viale Mazzini, 11/A and opens every day at 9:30 A.M. It is loaded with maps and wine itineraries that you can follow. When I visited, I was able to get a map of the Prosecco Wine Road, the highway that runs between Valdobbiadene and Conegliano. The information center also highlighted the wineries that were open for tours that day along with directions on how to drive there.

The Prosecco Wine Road, *La Strada del Prosecco,* is interesting to drive. While only 25 miles or 40 kilometers, it takes a lot longer than one hour or so because you're on a fairly narrow road in the hills. In my opinion, consider driving the full Prosecco Wine Road only if you have a fair amount of time.

But, before you leave Valdobbiadene, learn a bit more about Prosecco and this gorgeous wine region.

Prosecco Facts

Italian Prosecco is gaining in popularity, especially in the United States and Great Britain. Approximately 475 million bottles of Prosecco were made in 2016. 60 percent of all Prosecco is made in the Conegliano and Valdobbiadene area. The grape variety is named Glera. To be designated Prosecco Superiore, 85% must be made with the Glera grape.

In 2009, the Valdobbiadene-Conegliano region was designated DOCG, Denominazione di Origine Controllata e Garantita. This is the highest classification Italian wines can be awarded. It means that there are controlled production methods (controllata) and guaranteed wine quality (garantita) with each bottle. Only 25% of Prosecco is designated DOCG.

And, the best Prosecco is called Cartizze, after a small sub-region within Valdobbiadene considered the source of the finest Prosecco of all. The nearby villages of Saccol, Vidor and Santo Stefano historically have been the source of Cartizze. Cartizze (also known as Cartizze Superiore) is only produced in this sub-region and is considered the 'grand cru' of the region.

There are fewer than 200 wineries in this region so they are pretty much all small and many are family-owned. While that makes it a bit difficult to visit and taste wine, the Tourist Office in Valdobbiadene can help identify what wineries are open and how to get there.

I went to several wineries and highly recommend one of them. La Tordera is located in the village of Vidor, a short distance away from Valdobbiadene.

As you drive through the countryside, notice the steep terraces bursting with vineyards. I was there in October

Valdobbiadene and the Prosecco Wine Road

as families were harvesting and, while it was fascinating, that also meant that fewer wineries were open for tastings.

At various points along the drive, take a moment and take in the breathtaking views. This area is considered among the most scenic in Italy.

La Tordera Winery is in the village of Vidor that you passed through on the way to Valdobbiadene. The winery is 7 km away or about 11 minutes by car. The easiest way to get to the winery is to retrace your route from the town center. Get back on Via Erizzo/SP2 and SP34 to Via Ferret in Vidor. Continue on Via Ferret to reach La Tordera.

La Tordera Prosecco
Via Alnè Bosco, 23, 31020 Vidor
Phone: +39 0423 985362

This award-winning family winery is beautiful and my tour guide spoke several languages including English. Our tasting was delicious as well as educational.

The Cartizze is very special and I was delighted to be able to taste it. And, of course, purchase some!

According to 'Vinesse Wines" web site, "Prosecco is no longer the generic 'champagne' in brunch Bellinis."

'So noted Wine Spectator magazine, which added: "It's a wine that tipplers now order by name, a known quantity, distinct from other bubbles." La Tordera Brunei crafts an exceptional Prosecco made in a Brut style.'

Now that you've had a tasting of Prosecco and Cartizze Superiore, you may be interested in continuing on *La Strada del Prosecco or* the Valdobbiadene—Conegliano Wine Road.

La Strada del Prosecco

If so, leave the winery and head over to the village of Colbertaldo to get on the Wine Road (SP34).

Take Via Alnè Bosco to Via Roma in Vidor. Turn right onto Via Roma and follow Via Papa Luciani, Via Sentier and Via Calmentera to Via Montegrappa/SP34 in Mosnigo.

As you drive along SP34, you will pass through the villages of Refrontolo and Col San Martino that are particularly charming and may be places to stop for a while.

Continue on SP34, driving from Via Crevada into Conegliano.

Arriving in Conegliano via the Wine Road, you land in a somewhat industrial area. However, to understand its charms, you need to get to the historic center. The easiest way is to drive to the Conegliano train station on Via XXI Aprile. The train station is located on Piazza Aldo Moro.

One of the more famous Prosecco family wineries is located here.

Valdobbiadene and the Prosecco Wine Road

Carpenè Malvolti is one of the older and larger family-run Prosecco houses, and is located in the center of Conegliano. Its address is:

Carpenè Malvolti Winery
Via Antonio Carpenè, 1, 31015 Conegliano
Phone: +39 0438 364611
Hours: Monday–Friday, 9A.M.–12:30P.M, 2–6P.M.

To be honest, I did not actually get into Carpene Malvolti because I toured on a weekend. My research has indicated that it may be best to sign up for a tour ahead of time or at one of the local hotels in the town center.

To drive there, start from the train station on Piazza Aldo Moro. This is about a 3-5 minute drive. Head northwest on Viale Giosuè Carducci toward Corte delle Rose Turn right onto Via Giuseppe Mazzini, one of the main streets in Conegliano. Make a slight right turn onto Ponte San Martino and continue onto Piazzale S. Martino. Turn left onto Via Fenzi and then turn right onto Via Madonna. Shortly thereafter, turn left onto Via Antonio Carpenè and the Carpenè Malvolti Prosecco Winery is on your left.

Note: you can also visit this stunningly beautiful region starting from Conegliano. There is a train station in Conegliano and direct trains to/from Venezia and Treviso. Treviso is about 30 kilometers (19 mi) south by rail. Venezia is about a 50-minute train ride.

If you want to walk to the town center, park your car at the Parcheggio near the train station. Head northeast on Piazza Aldo Moro toward Via XXI Aprile.

Turn right. Walk to Via Verdi and turn left. Turn right onto Via Giuseppe Mazzini, one of the main streets in Conegliano and keep walking until you reach the center. It's about a 5-10 minute walk.

Enjoy your time in Conegliano, and return to your hotel after all this gorgeous scenery and sparklers, or, do what I did and head to Belluno.

> ### If You have the Time
>
> Belluno is Worth it.
>
> If you are interested in seeing the magnificent Dolomites more closely, consider driving from either Valdobbiadene or Conegliano to the stunning little town of Belluno, the Gateway to the Dolomites. It's about an hour's drive from either Valdobbiadene or Conegliano, and goes through extremely beautiful scenery. The routes are shown on the map of this tour #10.
>
> The major sights to see in Belluno, apart from the obvious Dolomiti Mountains surrounding the town as well as the Piave River that flows through it, are within walking distance from the central Piazza dei Martiri. The beautiful Basilica Cattedrale di San Martino and the Renaissance Palazzo dei Rittori, once the seat of Belluno's ruling Venetian government, are within easy walking distance.

My Favorite Restaurants in the Veneto

- **La Loggia Dining Room, Hotel Villa Michelangelo – Vicenza**
  Via Sacco 35, 36057 Arcugnano (Vicenza), +39 0444 550300
  A wonderful eighteenth-century Palladian-style country house hotel surrounded by a 5-acre park. This is a spectacular hotel that is extremely comfortable and elegant but not stuffy. Just outside Vicenza but a GPS is essential. The dining room is incredible. I stayed there and ate there several times during multiple visits and it's always memorable. Delectable Italian dishes beautifully presented and paired with wonderful local wines—it's really superb.

- **Hotel Villa Cipriani – Asolo**
  Via Canova 298, Asolo, TV 31011, +39 0423 523411
  To me, this is the real reason to visit Asolo. I had lunch here in September and it was incredible! Expensive, but worth it!! And dine in the gorgeous gardens if you can for an extra treat.

- **Garibaldi Vicenza**
  Piazza Dei Signori 1, 36100 Vicenza, +39 0444 325879
  Café Garibaldi—on Piazza dei Signori across from the basilica—fabulous atmosphere and wonderful casual food. Sitting on the terrace adjacent to the Piazza is dreamy. And of course join the crowd sipping Aperol Spritzers!

- **Ristorante Birreria Ottone**
  Bassano del Grappa
  Via Giacomo Matteotti, 50, 36061 Bassano Del Grappa, +39 0424 522206

Old style classic Italian restaurant in the center of Bassano. This is where the locals go (recommended by our innkeeper). The porcini risotto was delicious!

- **Caffe Pedrocchi - Padova**

    Via Otto Febbraio 1848 15, 35122, Padua, +39 049 878 1231

    What a wonderful historic café. It's stunning and has been the center of Padua's cultural life since it opened in 1841! Went there twice—sat inside one and outside as well---both wonderful. Good food, great coffee, reasonable in beautiful historic surroundings. And terrific courtly waiters who are only too pleased to give you the history.

- **Locandina Cappello - Verona**

    Via Cappello 16, 37121, Verona, +39 045 803 5218

    This is another 'local favorite'. This was highly recommended by our "California" local Veronese chefs but unfortunately we didn't make it. However, the reviews look fabulous and this will be on our list for the next visit.

About the Author
Janet Faulkner Chapman

Janet Faulkner Chapman lives in Marin County, in the San Francisco Bay Area, where she and her husband raised two children. She recently retired from a career in financial services, during which she held a variety of roles, including marketing, technology, risk, and data privacy/information security. She is a frequent traveler to Italy and other parts of the world.

www.ingramcontent.com/pod-product-compliance
Lightning Source LLC
Chambersburg PA
CBHW041503010526
44118CB00001B/6